KOREA

Jill DuBois

MARSHALL CAVENDISH

New York • London • Sydney

Reference edition reprinted 2000 by
Marshall Cavendish Corporation
99 White Plains Road
Tarrytown
New York 10591

© Times Media Private Limited 1996, 1994

Originated and designed by
Times Books International, an imprint of
Times Media Private Limited, a member of the
Times Publishing Group

Printed in Singapore

Library of Congress Cataloging-in-Publication Data:
DuBois, Jill.
    Korea / Jill DuBois.
      p. cm.—(Cultures Of The World)
    Includes bibliographical references and index.
    Summary: Explores the geography, history, people,
    economy, and lifestyles of Korea.
    ISBN 1-85435-582-1
    1. Korea—Juvenile literature [1. Korea.]
I. Title. II. Series.
DS902D83 1993
951.9—dc20   93–4381
              CIP
              AC

INTRODUCTION

AFTER CENTURIES OF DOMINATION by foreign powers, Korea has emerged from almost total destruction, following a divisive war, to take its place in the world economy. Divided in half after World War II, the country became the Republic of Korea south of the 38th parallel in 1948, and the Democratic People's Republic of Korea north of it.

South Korea (flag at top left) is a democratic nation and an industrial giant. Its people are guided by the ancient principles of Confucianism. North Korea is firmly Communist and economically hindered by a lack of foreign investment. The constitutions of both nations state the aim of reunification, but no one can predict whether the "Ireland of Asia" will eventually be unified.

As part of the *Cultures of the World* series, this book will familiarize you with the attitudes, lifestyles, and beliefs of the Koreans.

CONTENTS

Fish being dried on bamboo.

CONTENTS

**Ultramodern downtown
Seoul.**

GEOGRAPHY

THE KOREAN PENINSULA stretches southward from its neighbors, China and Russia, and lies between latitudes approximately the same as those of Vermont and South Carolina. It is surrounded by water on three sides: the Korea Bay and the Yellow Sea to the west, the Korea Strait to the south, and the Sea of Japan to the east. Along its coasts there are more than 3,000 islands.

Korea consists of two political units: the Democratic People's Republic of Korea (North Korea) and the Republic of Korea (South Korea), divided by a "Ceasefire Line" at north latitude 38°. Korea's total land area is 85,729 square miles (222,038 sq. km); about 55% is North Korea.

The name Korea comes from the Koryo dynasty (A.D. 918–1392). Koryo means "high and clear"—an appropriate description of the rugged mountains and clear rushing springs that characterize Korea's terrain.

Above: **Todam Sambong, Korea, at sunrise clearly illustrates why Korea is often called "The Land of the Morning Calm."**

Opposite: **Mt. Kumgang's Nine Dragons Waterfall in North Korea.**

TOPOGRAPHY

Korea's relief is dominated by mountains, from the Hamgyong Mountains in the north to the Taebaek Mountains that extend through South Korea.

The Taebaek mountain range is renowned for its beauty, particularly at Mount Sorak (Snow-Hill Mountain) and Mount Kumgang (Diamond Mountain).

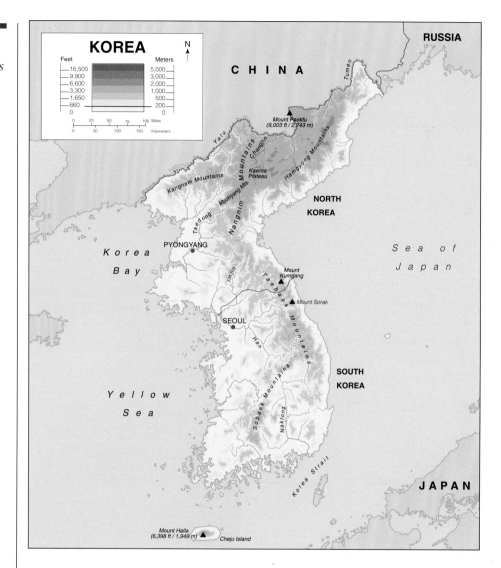

In the north, the Kaema plateau stretches from the center to the east. At its northeast tip is Korea's highest mountain, Mount Paektu (9,003 feet, 2,743 meters), an extinct volcano with a large crater lake. Smaller mountain ranges—the Nangnim and Myohyang Mountains in the center, the Kangnam Mountains in the northwest, and the southern Sobaek Mountains— abound throughout Korea. On Cheju, Korea's largest island, is South Korea's highest peak—Mount Halla, 6,398 feet (1,949 m) high.

RIVERS AND CRATER LAKES

Many of Korea's rivers are short and fast-flowing and drain into the Yellow Sea. The two longest rivers in North Korea begin at Mount Paektu; the Yalu runs 501 miles (806 km) westward to drain into Korea Bay, and the Tumen runs 324 miles (521 km) northeast to drain into the Sea of Japan. The Imjin is the main river shared by both North and South Korea. The principal rivers in South Korea are the Naktong (332 miles, 534 km), the Han, and the Kum. The Han and the Naktong are irrigation and industrial water suppliers.

Korea's two most famous lakes are volcanic crater lakes at Mount Paektu and Mount Halla. Although there is no volcanic activity on the peninsula, there are several hot springs and mineral springs. The waters are believed by many to cure or prevent numerous ailments such as indigestion, eczema, and rheumatism.

Yalu River, the longest in North Korea, flows along North Korea's border with China. Part of its course is lined by sentinel-like projections, the Chongun or "Thousand Soldiers" cliffs.

Cheju, a popular island vacation spot, is formed from the extinct volcano, Mount Halla, that rises 6,398 feet (1,949 m), above sea level.

COASTLINE AND ISLANDS

Korea's coastline is well indented with natural harbors in the south and west. There are few beaches along the eastern shore because the mountains run alongside it. Beaches are found where streams enter the sea.

More than 3,000 islands surround the Korean peninsula, most of which are off the southern and southwestern coasts. Except for the development of their fisheries in the 20th century, the islanders live as they have done for hundreds of years.

Cheju, meaning "the district over there," is Korea's largest island and is located approximately 60 miles (95 km) south of the peninsula. Cheju has a population of half a million. Its wealth comes from the sea and the export of citrus fruits. Home to palm trees, smooth beaches, caves, casinos, and golf courses, the island hosts more than 3 million tourists each year, making tourism one of its biggest sources of income. The inhabitants of Cheju consider themselves to be a subculture, as they are a matriarchal society, dominated by a large community of women spirit mediums.

CLIMATE

Korea experiences four seasons. Its temperate climate is characterized by monsoons in the summer, and cold and dry weather in the winter.

Summer (mid-June to mid-September) is hot, and the summer monsoon produces heavy rain that accounts for nearly 70% of the annual rainfall. In the south, temperatures fall between 75°F (24°C) and 85°F (29°C). This

An ancient temple of the Unified Silla period (1,300 years ago) covered in a blanket of snow.

type of weather is essential for growing rice; drier, cooler weather would cause crop failures. The north experiences cooler summers, when the average temperature is 68°F (20°C). Less rain falls in the north (24–40 inches, 60–100 cm a year) than in the south (40–55 inches, 100–140 cm).

Fall (mid-September to mid-November) is Korea's shortest season. Frosts begin to occur on October nights, but the days are often pleasantly clear and crisp, with temperatures of 55°F (13°C) to 65°F (18°C). The dry weather helps the rice crop ripen and permits the farmers to harvest it. Winter crops such as wheat and barley are planted during fall.

Winter (mid-November to March) is cold and dry but not too severe in the south, so rice and barley can be grown as the days are warm. There is snow but it only accounts for 5% (northern Korea) to 10% (southern Korea) of the annual precipitation. In North Korea winter is bitterly cold, with temperatures ranging from 21°F (–6°C) to –8°F (–22°C), the lower extreme being typical of the northern interior.

Spring (April to mid-June) is a short season, when the thaw begins and rainfall increases.

THE ELIXIR OF LIFE

Insam ("in-SUM," meaning ginseng), Korea's oldest export product, is considered an "elixir of life" or a cure-all. Many positive effects have been attributed to this root, from strengthening one's mental powers to enhancing one's love life.

The use of ginseng dates as far back as 3000 B.C., when it grew abundantly in Mongolia, northern China, and Korea. Popularity and aggressive harvesting in Korea made it scarce about a thousand years ago, so cultivation was encouraged throughout the southern provinces, where it continues to flourish to this day. South Korea is the world's leading provider of ginseng root.

Growing ginseng root is a very involved process. Seeds are planted in a mixture of oak and chestnut leaves and shielded from sunlight in long rows of thatched shelters. The entire growth cycle takes from four to six years. Once harvested, the roots are washed, peeled, steamed, and dried. They are sorted according to age and quality.

Ginseng comes in two varieties: *hong* ("hohng," red) and *baek* ("back," white). The white variety is less expensive and is readily available in Korea and throughout the world. White ginseng is believed to be adequate for general health if it is taken continuously over a long period of time. The red variety, though, is considered to be more potent. It is very expensive and is cultivated mainly for export as it is in great demand. East Asians use it for the weak, the elderly, or people in poor health.

Recent studies have confirmed its usefulness as a general tonic but have not identified the useful medical properties in either variety. It is thought that ginseng affects the central nervous system, producing results such as increased mental awareness and stamina, and improved appetite.

A serious user puts the whole root into a glass, covers it with a favorite liquor, and waits until its curative powers seep into the liquid before drinking it. Ginseng is available in modern products ranging from pills to chewing gum, teas to shampoo. It is still considered most effective when steeped in a liquid such as tea. Ginseng tea houses are found throughout Korea.

FLORA

Although the climate and land make it possible for extensive forests with a variety of trees to grow, a good portion of the woodlands have disappeared. This is because of erosion from torrential rains, defoliation caused by the Korean War, and the need for fuel and timber. Tremendous reforestation efforts have been taking place since the late 1960s; trees that will contribute to future timber needs are generally selected for planting.

Common trees are the many varieties of pine, maple, oak, poplar, birch, and willow. In the northern mountains, fir, spruce, larch, pine, and Korean cedar are commonly found. Reeds and sedges grow wild in stony lowland areas that are subject to flooding. Many herbs and roots (the most well-known being ginseng) are native to Korea, where herbal medicine is widely practiced.

Korea's flowering plants include camellias, lilac, forsythia, chrysanthemum, rose, and azaleas. The hills are bright pink with azaleas in early spring and these flowers are often depicted in Korean art and poetry. Korea's national flower is the Rose of Sharon, a species of hardy hibiscus that grows back when cut down and has a long growing season. It symbolizes Korea's strength in adversity.

Fruit trees also flourish in Korea. Apples, pears, peaches, tangerines, persimmons, figs, and cherries are abundant. Native nuts grown include pine nuts, chestnuts, walnuts, and gingko nuts. In the warmer, sub-tropical climate on Cheju, bananas and pineapples are grown.

A rush mat being woven.

13

FAUNA

More than 350 species of birds have been recorded in Korea. Native birds include the crow, heron, crane, swallow, robin, magpie, and oriole. Migratory birds include ducks, teals, swans, and geese. Two favorite birds of the Koreans are the crane, which is considered a good luck symbol and often depicted in art, and the black and white magpie. If the magpie is seen early in the morning, Koreans expect to hear good news as the day progresses.

Animals found in Korea include the bear, deer, wildcat, wolf, weasel, badger, leopard, and many smaller mammals. Chin Island, off the southwest coast, breeds a unique domesticated wolf called the chindo dog.

CITIES

Korea's most populated cities are Seoul (11 million), Pusan (4 million), Taegu (2.5 million), and Inchon (2 million) in South Korea; and Pyongyang (2 million), Hamhung (680,000), and Chongjin (550,000) in North Korea.

SEOUL This metropolis on the Han River ranks as one of the 10 largest cities in the world. The capital city of South Korea

THE PALACES OF SEOUL

The spirit of the Yi dynasty kings, who ruled the country for more than 500 years, still lives in Seoul, for it is there that the only palaces of Korea remain.

Korean palaces are not single structures as they are in Europe. They are huge collections of buildings, with gardens, pagodas, magnificent reception halls, and tiled roofs with sweeping eaves. They are modelled after palaces in China, although they have distinctive Korean features.

Three of Seoul's four existing palaces are in the northern part of the city, strategically placed with their backs to the mountains which served as a natural barrier to invaders from the north. They face south to capture the rays of the sun in the winter as well as to avoid the evil spirits that were thought to blow in from the northeast. The fourth palace is in the center of the capital city and is much smaller than the others. Seoul's palaces have been partially rebuilt over the years. They are a source of national pride, and the government plans to restore them to their original splendor.

functions as its political, economic, educational, and cultural hub. Seoul has served as the Korean capital since the Yi dynasty, more than 500 years ago. Just a few steps away from the ultramodern hotels in the heart of the city are public palace grounds.

A 10 mile (16 km) wall was built around Seoul hundreds of years ago, with nine gates providing entrance to the city. Four of these gates have been destroyed over the years.

PUSAN Pusan is South Korea's largest port and second-largest city. The fishing industry is also based there. With about 4 million inhabitants, it has tremendous industrial activity, yet it is one of Korea's most popular resort cities because of its historical landmarks, beaches, and hot mineral springs.

Opposite, top: **Cranes are a favorite bird of Koreans, as they are believed to bring good luck.**

Opposite, bottom: **The city of Seoul blends the new and the old.**

Panmunjom in the Demilitarized Zone clearly shows the division of Korea, with North Korean guards on one side of the line and United Nations guards on the other.

PANMUNJOM Panmunjom is the site of Korean War truce talks between North Korean and United Nations negotiators, and the reunification talks since the ceasefire in 1953. It is located on the western end of the border that separates North and South Korea. This border, about 2¹/₂ miles (4 km) wide and stretching 152 miles (245 km) from the Sea of Japan to the Yellow Sea, is referred to as the "Ceasefire Line" or Demilitarized Zone (DMZ).

Panmunjom, once a farming village obliterated in the Korean War, has become the focal point of what one writer called "the most ruthless border on earth, separating the opposing elements of a single country." Bus tours run from Seoul to Panmunjom, although no visitors are allowed when reunification talks are under way. Those who have been there report that it is a very moving experience, for it emphasizes the two Koreas' inability to strike an agreement and reunite their people.

TAEGU The third largest urban center in Korea is Taegu, home of the Talsong Fortress built by ancient rulers more than 3,000 years ago. Although Taegu was once known as a market city, specializing in apples and medicinal herbs, it is now an important industrial center and Korea's largest textile producer. Taegu is also an educational center, the location of five colleges and four universities.

INCHON The port and industrial city of Inchon is located near Seoul and, during the summer, it is a popular getaway spot because of its beautiful beaches. The tidal range in the harbor is 60 feet (18 m), the second highest in the world. Near Inchon is Kanghwa Island, Korea's fifth largest island, famous for its historical sites.

KYONGJU This ancient city, the site of kings' tombs, sacred pagodas, and Buddhist temples, is Korea's museum-without-walls. It was the capital of the Silla dynasty, which flourished from 57 B.C. to A.D. 917. In 1973, archeologists unearthed more than 10,000 items in a Silla burial chamber, which is now called the Heavenly Horse Tomb. The thousands of exceptional historical treasures that enhance the Kyongju valley have prompted the United Nations Education, Scientific, and Cultural Organization (U.N.E.S.C.O.) to name Kyongju one of the world's 10 most important ancient cities.

The Koryo Hotel in Pyongyang is one of the city's most modern structures.

PYONGYANG After most of the cities of North Korea were razed to the ground in the Korean War, they were rebuilt with greater attention paid to function than to architectural merit. North Korea's capital city and financial center is the exception. Among its many landmarks are a modern subway, a sports stadium, and a 105-story hotel. The city is believed to have been established in 2333 B.C. as the capital of Choson (Korea) by Tangun, the legendary figure who, in folk belief, founded Korea.

HISTORY

IN 3000 B.C. KOREA was known as Choson, meaning "Land of the Morning Calm." Two legends account for the founding of Choson. The first says that the ancient state was established by a godlike figure called Tangun ("CHANG-goon") in the area that is now Pyongyang. Tangun is credited with uniting the various tribes inhabiting the area around 2333 B.C. The Tangun era, known as Ancient Choson, lasted about 1,200 years. National Foundation Day or Tangun Day is celebrated annually on October 3.

Above: **"Guards" at the Pulguk-sa Temple.**

Opposite: **A stone Buddha in the Sokkuram grotto, situated in a cave behind the historic Pulguk-sa Temple in Kyongju. Built in the eighth century, it is considered by scholars to be the most beautiful Buddhist sculpture in Asia.**

The other prominent legend, supported in part by ancient Chinese texts, honors a Manchu tribal chieftain named Kija, who led a band of his supporters to Choson after the fall of the Chinese Shang dynasty around 1100 B.C. He and his Manchurian successors then ruled the conquered territory until 194 B.C.

Whatever the favored myth for the origin of Korean culture, archeologists have determined that some prehistoric peoples of the Altaic language group probably migrated to the Korean peninsula from Siberia, Manchuria, and Mongolia (in Northern and Central Asia). These early peoples were hunters, fishermen, and farmers who worshiped the gods and spirits of nature in a belief system called shamanism. Their religious beliefs and practices have remained in Korea through five millennia.

Chinese influence on Korean art can be seen in this fourth or fifth century painting of a hunting scene. It was discovered in a tomb in Koguryo, in present-day North Korea.

ANCIENT HISTORY

The wandering tribes that entered the Korean peninsula found people (referred to as Paleoasians) already living there. The cultural development of these early native peoples was influenced by developments in China. Chinese models of civilization and government helped form ancient Korea, or Choson. In 108 B.C. the Chinese had a more direct impact on Korean cultural development when the Han dynasty conquered the northern half of the peninsula and established four territories there. Korea's recorded history began with this event.

Korean tribes recaptured three of the four territories in 75 B.C. The remaining territory, Lalang, remained under Chinese control. It was through the flourishing Chinese colony of Lalang that the characteristics of Chinese civilization—such as the system of writing, ideas on religion, governmental systems, and the art of iron working—were transmitted to the various Korean peoples.

THE THREE KINGDOMS

By the first century A.D. three Korean states were in existence: Silla was founded in 57 B.C., Koguryo in 37 B.C., and Paekche in 18 B.C.

Nearest China was the Koguryo kingdom, created when several tribes united in the northeastern region of the peninsula. Initially the most powerful of the three kingdoms, it established its capital at Pyongyang. The Paekche kingdom was founded by tribes that migrated southward to avoid the aggression of Koguryo warriors. Eventually these tribes occupied southern Korea, establishing their capital initially near Seoul. The Silla kingdom, the most aristocratic of the three kingdoms, established its capital at Kyongju.

The three kingdoms endured from 57 B.C. to A.D. 668. During that time, Buddhism was adopted and Confucianism was introduced by visitors from China.

In 618, the Tang dynasty came to power in China. Its rulers were eager to expand their sphere of influence. Capitalizing on hostilities among the three kingdoms, they helped Silla to gain control of the peninsula. Paekche was conquered in 660 and Koguryo in 668. The Tang rulers had deceived themselves, however, in thinking they could eventually gain control over Silla. Silla encouraged revolts in the conquered territories of Paekche and Koguryo, then defeated the Chinese troops sent to quell the revolts. Eventually, China agreed to recognize Silla as an independent state.

With this victory, Silla was able to spread its cultural influence throughout Choson. During the Unified Silla, the peninsula was finally united and under the influence of a Korean government.

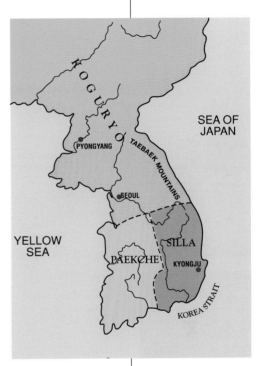

Territories on the Korean peninsula controlled by the early kingdoms of Silla, Koguryo, and Paekche around A.D. 600.

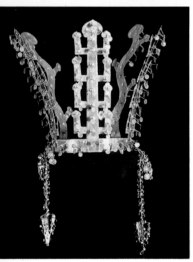

Many gold ornaments of the Silla period reveal the artistry of Silla craftsmen, admired even today.

UNIFIED SILLA PERIOD (668–917)

The Unified Silla period is often referred to as Korea's "golden age of art and culture." Beautiful temples and shrines were built during this period, and the complicated Chinese writing system used in Korea was simplified, allowing for a wide variety of writers. The arts blossomed, and Choson became a great Asian center for architecture, painting, ceramics, music, and the production of lacquerware, ironware, and gold and silver jewelry.

Other notable accomplishments of the Unified Silla period were land reforms that benefited the poor, the development of irrigation systems that improved rice cultivation, and the establishment of a national university. The economy flourished as trade between East Asian nations grew. Remains of temples, tombs, pagodas, and artifacts found in Kyongju, the Silla capital, reveal the remarkable accomplishments of this period.

Unified Silla started to decline around 780 when infighting among nobles began. Finally, after many violent clashes, Wang Kon, the leader of a separatist faction, gained control over Koguryo, then Paekche, and finally Silla. Wang Kon proclaimed himself leader of a new state in 918 and established a capital at Songdo (modern-day Kaesong, just west of Panmunjom). He called his nation Koryo, a shortened form of Koguryo, from which the modern name of Korea is derived. A capable leader, Wang Kon was renamed Taejo, which means "first king," after his death.

KORYO DYNASTY (918–1392)

Korean culture thrived during the 11th century. Buddhism flourished through heavy Koryo patronage and became a powerful force in politics and culture. Buddhist scholars produced writings and art, and numerous temples and pagodas were erected. Valuable celadon pottery was created, as was a form of poetry known as *sijo* ("SAE-jo"). A notable Korean

invention of the 11th century was moveable metal type, which had a major impact on the spread of literacy and culture, and came a full two centuries before Gutenberg developed moveable type in Germany.

In the later Koryo period, the influence of Confucianism was enhanced. The aristocrats believed in Buddhism as a religion, but looked to Confucianism for political and ethical guidance. Schools teaching Confucianism were built alongside the Buddhist temples.

Koryo was continually harassed by northern tribes. In 1231 the Mongols invaded Korea. The state was then under the power of the successors of General Choe Chung-hon, who had established military rule in 1170. After 30 years of resistance, the Choes were overthrown by Koryo civilians, who concluded a peace treaty with the Mongols. The Mongols interfered in the country's politics from time to time, but otherwise observed the treaty.

By that time the Koryo kingdom was beset by other problems. The majority of the land was owned by aristocrats and farmed by tenants who were heavily taxed. Some tenants sold themselves as servants in order to pay the exorbitant taxes. In addition, the government, dissatisfied with the Buddhist leaders, had recruited a new group of scholar-officials who were advocates of Neo-Confucianism. The new group became disillusioned when the government could not compensate them amply.

A new leader arose to meet the challenges facing the government; General Yi Songgye took over leadership in a peaceful coup in 1392. Although the new dynasty was officially given the name of Choson, it was widely known as the Yi dynasty.

Part of the collection of 81,258 wooden blocks with Buddhist scriptures carved on them, the world's oldest and most complete set of Buddhist scriptures. This 13th century project took 16 years to complete and can be seen at the Haein Temple near Taegu.

23

Homage being paid at the shrine containing the memorial tablets of the Yi dynasty kings. This ritual is performed on the first Sunday in May, in Seoul.

YI DYNASTY (1392–1910)

Yi realized that reforms were necessary if his reign was to be successful. He restructured the government and based it on Confucian concepts, emphasizing respect for elders and ancestors. Books on Confucian classics and literature were printed to encourage higher learning. Some of the ceremonies introduced in the dynasty are still practiced in Korea today.

Under his rule, land was redistributed and Buddhist temples were closed. The capital was moved to Hanyang (Seoul), where Yi's government, a small group of nobles, remained for more than 500 years. Like Wong Kon, Yi was given the title of Taejo after his death.

Sejong (1418–1450), the fourth ruler of the Yi dynasty, showed tremendous concern for the ethics of Confucianism. Rigid class distinctions were firmly established during his reign in an attempt to create an ideal Confucian state. The importance of proper conduct between the individual and the family, and the individual and the state were especially emphasized.

Sejong was considered the greatest Yi dynasty king. Under his rule there were developments in technology, science, philosophy, and music. A major achievement was to supervise the creation of *hangul* ("HAHN-gool"), a phonetic alphabet that could easily be used by the masses because of its simplicity. Soon after Sejong's reign, the country fell under siege again. The Mongols presented a persistent threat at the border, and the Japanese raided the coast relentlessly.

THE IMJIN WAR

In the late 1500s, Japan, under the powerful military leader Toyotomi Hideyoshi, invaded Korea in the Imjin War. Japan overwhelmed Korea with tremendous manpower, capturing Pusan, Seoul, and Pyongyang. The period 1592–1598 was one of great devastation as a result of the Imjin War.

A replica of the "turtle-boat," the ironclad ship with which Admiral Yi Sunsin defeated the Japanese, can be found at the Chunhae Naval Academy.

With help from China, the Koreans finally forced the Japanese out. Were it not for the brilliance of Admiral Yi Sunsin, the inventor of the "turtleboat," an ironclad ship, Korea might have suffered total defeat. As it was, farmland was destroyed, and artisans and technicians were captured and taken to Japan. With the loss of some of Korea's finest minds, and the ravages of war, Korea became a weak and unproductive state.

Chinese aggression in the early 1600s found a powerless Korea willing to pay great sums of money to prevent war. After its unfortunate encounters with foreign powers, Korea separated itself from all nations except China, and became known as the Hermit Kingdom. The self-enforced isolation brought Korean society to a standstill, while other nations experienced a rich period of intellectual achievement.

China continued to have a stranglehold on the Korean government until Japan defeated China in the Sino-Japanese War of 1894–1895. Russia and Japan then competed for influence in Korea until Japan's victory in the Russo-Japanese War (1904–1905), which resulted in the Japanese annexation of Korea in 1910. A new, highly oppressive era began.

JAPANESE RULE

After Korea's annexation in 1910, Korean businesses and landholdings were taken over by Japanese citizens with the help of the new government. The Japanese modernized the country by building roads, dams, railroads, and ports, and by exploiting Korea's natural resources. Koreans were forced to adopt Japanese names and participate in Japanese religious rituals. The Korean language was prohibited from being taught or even spoken in schools.

Japan's oppressive rule motivated a historically complacent people to stage demonstrations in order to win worldwide support for their independence. The effort, called *Samil,* was staged after the Korean delegation at the Versailles Conference (the international talks held following World War I) failed to gain approval for self-rule in 1919. Major protests were held throughout the country.

Unhappy about these displays, the Japanese sent in forces to quell the revolts. As many as 7,000 Koreans are thought to have been killed in the violence that ensued.

A DIVIDED KOREA

The entrance to the secret gardens where Korean royalty stayed until the Japanese ended the Yi dynasty.

When the Allies emerged the victors at the end of World War II, the fate of the Korean peninsula was in new hands. In the midst of the Cold War, neither the United States nor the Soviet Union wanted the other to take control of the entire country. The Soviet Union pushed for a Communist government, while the United States insisted on a democratic, capitalist

system. It was agreed that the Soviet Union would accept the Japanese surrender north of the 38th parallel, while American troops would remain south of it until a plan was developed to reunite Korea. Since no agreement could be reached after two years, the United States turned the problem over to the United Nations.

The United Nations' solution was to hold a free election so that Koreans could decide on the issue. The Soviet Union refused entry to the UN Commission meant to oversee the election, so an election was held only in the southern half of the country in 1948.

In July 1948, Syngman Rhee won the presidency. The Republic of Korea was formed south of the 38th parallel in August, and its National Assembly drew up a constitution. Shortly thereafter, the Soviet Union announced the formation of the Democratic People's Republic of Korea with Kim Il Sung, a Korean Communist general, as government leader. Both governments claimed to represent the whole country.

Above: **Former South Korean President Roh Tae-woo, an army general. The Korean War created a breed of military politicians in both North and South Korea.**

Opposite: **Soldiers near Mount Paektu. North Korea has invested heavily in its military.**

THE KOREAN WAR

In June 1950 the North Korean armed forces attacked South Korea in an attempt to unify the country. This event marked the beginning of the Korean War.

American soldiers entered the war in September but were forced to retreat to the southeast corner. Subsequently a United Nations force of men from 16 nations was sent to support South Korea against northern aggression. The UN forces moved into the north, close to the Chinese border, when China suddenly entered the conflict in support of the Communists. A stalemate resulted with armies positioned at the middle of the Korean peninsula.

A ceasefire was signed in July 1953, but so far there has been no peace treaty.

EFFECTS OF WAR South Korea eventually gained about 1,500 square miles (3,885 sq. km) of territory. Seoul was nearly leveled, and cropland throughout South Korea was ravaged. North Korea suffered as well, with its population reduced by more than one and a half to two million, or nearly 12% of the total.

Political differences keep the two Koreas separated today. North Korea remains steadfastly Communist while South Korea is firmly capitalist. Given such opposite ideals, there seems to be little room for negotiation.

IN QUEST OF PEACEFUL UNIFICATION

In 1972 the two Koreas jointly announced that they would open dialogue for peaceful reunification. During the 20 years that followed, the tension between them rose and negotiations progressed at a painfully slow pace, sometimes with intervals of years between meetings.

Political observers have questioned the sincerity of North Korea's intended "peaceful unification." They point to incidents of hostility, including North Korea's dispatch of armed ships into South Korean waters, the discovery of three tunnels dug by North Koreans under the demilitarized zone, the discovery, by satellite, of secret nuclear sites that led to suspicions that North Korea may be developing nuclear arms, and the bombing of a South Korean jetliner.

North Korea, on the other hand, claims that the "Team Spirit" military exercises conducted by the United States and South Korea are not compatible with peaceful dialogue.

What is the probability of unification? For 47 years now, the two Koreas have been guided by opposing ideologies. Those skeptical of unification point out that the North has laid down unacceptable preconditions concerning the form of government, and the domestic and foreign policy of a unified Korea. The longer they dawdle, the further apart the two countries grow. The heavy cost of German unification—with its strikes, unemployment, and rising taxes—has sobered once enthusiastic South Korean advocates of unification. Now they warn that hasty unification could set back South Korea's booming economy for years. Now they think that perhaps the unification process should not be rushed.

GOVERNMENT

A PRESIDENT IS HEAD OF STATE in both North and South Korea. The similarity ends there, for while the South Korean president can only be elected for a single five-year term, the North Korean president, Kim Il Sung, held power from 1945 until his death in 1994, and has been succeeded by his son, Kim Jong Il.

THE CONSTITUTION

SOUTH KOREA South Korea's Constitution was adopted in 1948, and has been revised nine times. It allows for three branches of government: the executive headed by the president, the National Assembly, and the judiciary. The president is elected for a single five-year term. He can appoint or dismiss a prime minister (with the National Assembly's approval) as well as ministers and heads of office. He is both head of foreign relations and commander-in-chief of the armed forces.

NORTH KOREA In 1972 North Korea adopted a Constitution promoting *juche* ("CHOO-cheh"), meaning self-reliance. North Korea's trade relations are restricted to Communist or politically nonaligned countries, so it has had to learn to be self-sufficient.

There are three branches of government: the Supreme People's Assembly, the Central People's Committee, and the Administration Council responsible for the ministries. The president is elected for a four-year term by the Supreme People's Assembly and may be re-elected.

Above: **A poster in North Korea promoting the idea of *juche* or self-reliance. The Korean caption at the bottom means "Long Live The Great Juche Idea!"**

Opposite: **Government building in Seoul.**

31

APRIL SHOWERS BRING ...

One Korean tradition that originated in the Yi dynasty is scholars' responsibility to act as government watchdogs. To observe this tradition, every spring, students and police challenge each other at the gates of the universities.

Since the state of South Korea was created in 1948, students have represented the country's conscience in matters of human rights and democracy. Their protests have been effective. In 1960 student uprisings forced the resignation of the authoritarian Syngman Rhee. In 1987, extensive student riots caused the military government to write a constitution that called for a democratic election for president. These uprisings often turned into bloodbaths.

From the late 1980s until 1990 democratic reforms were pursued as a substitute to the violent riots. But in 1990, just when officials started to believe that the springtime ritual might be a thing of the past, a student protesting a tuition hike was killed by riot police, sparking violent demonstrations across the nation's campuses. Twelve people set themselves on fire to demonstrate their loathing of the government.

GOVERNMENT

South Korea's lawmaking body is the National Assembly. Voters elect two-thirds of the members to serve four-year terms. The remaining third are represented proportionately by political parties winning five or more seats in the election. Some of the functions of this body are to propose, reject, or approve legislative bills; to ratify foreign treaties; to confirm or reject the appointment of the prime minister; and to oversee administrative agencies.

North Korea's most powerful body is the Supreme People's Assembly. Voters elect its members to serve four-year terms. Some of its functions are to adopt or amend legal enactments; to determine state policy; to elect the president and members of the Central People's Committee; to elect the prime minister and legal officials on the president's recommendation; to approve the state budget; to decide on matters of war and peace; and to elect members of the Standing Committee, which votes on bills and amends legislation when the Supreme People's Assembly is not in session.

ARMED FORCES

South Korea's military strength consists of an army of more than half a million, a navy, and an air force. There is also a civilian defense force of about 3.5 million. Military service is compulsory for between 30 and 36 months. South Korea's defense expenditure is 5% of its gross national product (GNP).

Although North Korea's official defense expenditure is 12%, it is suspected that the figure could be as high as 25% of GNP. Its military strength consists of an army, a navy, and an air force. In addition to this, there are 200,000 security and border guards, a workers' army (called "Red Guards") of about 4 million, and a youth army of about 700,000. National military service is five to eight years in the army, five to 10 years in the navy, or three to four years in the air force.

Smartly dressed in their white uniforms, these navy men are among the 50,000 who defend South Korea's waters.

TWO KIMS OF THE SOUTH

Although Kim is the most common surname in Korea, every South Korean knows just who you mean if you mention the two Kims. They are Kim Young-sam (right), the President, and Kim Dae-jung, South Korea's most influential political leaders. As contenders for the Korean presidency, they split the opposition votes in the 1987 election, paving the way for Roh Tae-woo. But Kim Young-sam won the election in 1992.

The two Kims followed unusual paths for politicians. Kim Dae-jung, perhaps the country's most famous dissident, has been exiled, jailed, and even sentenced to death in the course of his career.

Kim Young-sam spent years under house arrest for opposing South Korea's authoritarian rule. He even staged a 23-day hunger strike to attain greater civil liberties from the government. In an election that marked a milestone in a country that had long struggled to be a democracy, Kim Young-sam emerged the victor. In the 1992 election there were no serious accusations of vote fraud, intimidation at the polls, or counting irregularities.

SOUTH KOREA'S MARCH TO DEMOCRACY

Syngman Rhee, South Korea's first president, promised to introduce democracy in a state marked by repression. Instead his was a weak and corrupt government that eventually led to nationwide student protests, forcing Rhee to step down in 1960. In 1961 General Park Chung Hee proclaimed martial law. Soon after, demands for a civilian government prompted his retirement from the military. He ran again in the 1963 presidential election as a civilian, and won. Under his leadership, the Constitution was changed to increase presidential power and remove statutes limiting terms in office. Freedom of speech and of the press were severely restricted after 1972 because Park feared that criticism would weaken the state. He was assassinated in 1979.

The military took control of the government after the assassination. Attempts to restore constitutional rights caused violent clashes between the military and demonstrators. In 1980 General Chun Doo-hwan, the leader of the military action against the demonstrators, took control. Chun's presidency was marked by student demonstrations for the reinstatement of direct elections.

In 1987, Roh Tae-woo, another former general, won the election. Because he was a major participant in the 1979 military coup, many questioned his commitment to democracy.

In December 1992, Roh Tae-woo was replaced by Kim Young-sam, a leader committed to democracy. The 1992 presidential election was the fairest in South Korea's history.

LEADERS OF THE NORTH

A personality cult surrounds the two Kims of North Korea, known there as the Great Leader (the late President Kim Il Sung, who died in 1994) and the Dear Leader (Kim Il Sung's son, Kim Jong Il, who succeeded his father).

Kim Jong Il (right) was named his father's successor in 1980 and had been preparing for the role since then. He was appointed to a key position in the Korean Workers Party, which his detractors allege was deliberate, allowing him to remove those from the party who opposed his succession. Kim Jong Il's birthday was declared a public holiday in 1985. In March 1993, he was appointed supreme commander of the military, a post traditionally held by the president.

There is no doubt that Kim Jong Il is ambitious. He surrounds himself with technocrats who influence the economic strategy in North Korea. Foreign analysts call him a terrorist, the mastermind of the 1983 bomb attack in Rangoon, Burma (Yangon, Myanmar) that killed members of the South Korean cabinet, but this has never been conclusively proved.

POLITICAL PARTIES

The ruling party in South Korea is the Democratic Liberal Party, headed by its chairman, Kim Young-sam, who has been the country's president since 1992. The main opposition party is the Democratic Party, which holds seats in the National Assembly. The Peace and Democracy Party was a prominent political player before 1992, but its head, Kim Dae-jung, retired after he lost the 1992 election.

Communist North Korea has one major political party, the Korean Workers Party. All the other political organizations are affiliated to it, leaving little room for political opposition.

Opposite: **Kim Young-sam, elected president in the December 1992 polls, the most honest in South Korea's history.**

Above: **Kim Jong Il, North Korea's president, waving to the crowd of supporters who have come to see their Dear Leader.**

ECONOMY

SINCE THE KOREAN WAR, South Korea has become a major player in the international economic arena. Before 1960, few of its industries were developed and the nation had few natural resources on which to rely. The division of the country into two separate states disrupted domestic trading patterns and left South Korea without access to mineral resources. Despite all that, South Korea has grown into a world producer of steel, iron, automobiles, ships, and electronics. The rapid economic progress in the past two decades is beginning to stall, yet South Korea remains a great success story.

The economic picture in North Korea is the reverse. At first, North Korea's economy grew rapidly because of available resources and the Communist government's ability to marshal the people to work. When the economy became more complex, the government's rigid control over economic matters lowered efficiency.

Today the economy is beset by problems, one of which is a lack of human resources. Losses suffered in the Korean War and the maintenance of large reserves of armed forces has worsened the labor shortage.

In the mid-1980s, North Korea changed its policy and began encouraging joint ventures with foreign companies. By 1989 the first joint venture with China—a marine fishery products enterprise—was achieved. So far, attempts to acquire Western capital and technology have been largely unsuccessful.

Opposite: **The Pohang Iron and Steel Company in South Korea is one of the largest steel producers in Asia. Yet, because of the great demand for steel created by South Korea's vehicle and electronics industries, the country still has to import steel.**

Below: **A fishing town north of Wonsan on the east coast of North Korea.**

Workmen at a dock in Pusan.

INDUSTRIES IN SOUTH KOREA

MANUFACTURING   Manufacturing accounts for 75% of industrial production in South Korea. Although nearly all of South Korea's industries are privately owned, there is often cooperation between government and private businesses. Sometimes the government develops new industries itself and then slowly privatizes them, at other times it offers incentives for entrepreneurs to begin new businesses. This type of close cooperation between private business and the government has led to the rise of huge business groups, known in Korea as *chaebol* ("JAE-bull").

One well-known *chaebol* is Hyundai, a 45-year-old enterprise consisting of more than 20 companies that produce automobiles, ships, furniture, and computer chips, among other things. Hyundai and South Korea's three other large *chaebol* (Lucky-Goldstar, Daewoo, and Samsung) contribute to more than half of the nation's GNP.

In the last two decades, production of electronic goods such as television sets, appliances, and computer chips has developed so significantly that South Korea is now a world competitor. Machinery and ships also play a major role in industrial manufacturing.

MINING South Korea's principal minerals include coal, gold, silver, tungsten, talc, and iron ore. Limits on natural resources have prompted the development of overseas mining interests to meet the country's needs.

CONSTRUCTION South Korea's burgeoning economy has created a construction boom. Buildings, roads, and sewer systems are being built to keep pace with the progress. South Korean construction workers, known for their skill, are also active in building projects abroad, particularly in the Middle East, Latin America, Africa, and Southeast Asia.

A tremendous construction boom has resulted from the economic development of South Korea.

INDUSTRIES IN NORTH KOREA

MANUFACTURING North Korea manufactures machinery for domestic industries, such as agriculture and the armed forces. Metal-cutting machines, tractors, weapons, and army vehicles are some examples of North Korea's products, but since the quality of the machines is often poor, the country also imports equipment from Western countries.

MINING About 80%–90% of the important mineral deposits of the peninsula are in North Korean territory. The most important ones include coal, iron ore, lead, zinc, tungsten, and fluorite. The principal coal mines are located north of Pyongyang. More than half of the nation's electricity output is generated by coal-powered plants. Iron ore is a major export item, followed by steel, lead, zinc, and cement.

AGRICULTURE, FISHING, AND FORESTRY

SOUTH KOREA As recently as the 1950s, agriculture represented about 40% of the GNP and 70% of employment. By the early 1990s, agriculture had declined to 7.5% of the GNP, and employed only 14% of South Korea's workforce. Despite this drastic drop, there are still approximately 2 million small farms, the majority of which are privately owned and engaged in rice cultivation.

South Korea is one of the world's leading fishing nations, with a fleet of more than 800 deep-sea vessels. Many efforts have been made to expand the fishing industry because fish is the leading source of protein in the Korean diet, and it is a fine export commodity. Besides the deep-sea fleet, many thousands of coastal boats work the waters around South Korea where there is an abundance of fish and shellfish.

NORTH KOREA North Korea has high-quality timber on its mountains, where extensive forests of larch, spruce, fir, and pine support the timber industry. The local forests cannot provide all of the country's needs, however, so the country imports timber from Russia.

About 80% of North Korea is mountainous, so most of its farms are located in the plains of the western region. After World War II, land was

SAEMAUL UNDONG

After the Korean War, cities began developing rapidly. In the rural villages, however, poverty was so overwhelming that President Park Chung Hee launched a revitalization program to bring the farmers' economic level up to that of urban workers.

The program was called *Saemaul Undong* ("SU-mil Oon-DONG"), or the New Community Movement. Launched in 1971, it was designed to help farmers reach a new level of productivity and improve their lives in the process. The townspeople gathered together to brainstorm over the needs of villages. A leader was elected to devise a plan of action, and once the plan was organized, the government provided materials, while the people did the work. It showed the people in the farming communities that through diligence and a cooperative spirit they could accomplish their goals and prosper.

The New Community Movement was such a success that similar programs were created for larger towns. *Saemaul Undong* programs encouraged citizens to live within their means, keep family rituals simple, and eliminate waste.

The program's success was so greatly admired that visitors from more than 100 countries came to study the program firsthand. It is difficult for other societies to duplicate such a program, however, because it is an idea so wrapped up in Korean thought, philosophy, and values that it may not work in other lands. Although this movement was successful for the first 10 years, its effectiveness declined after 1980.

redistributed to the peasants. This reduced the size of the already small farms. After the Korean War, the drive for collective farms was intensified, and in the 1980s North Korea had nearly 4,000 cooperative or state-owned farms. About 37% of the working population are currently engaged in agriculture, and the two most important crops are rice and corn. Farms are well mechanized with ploughing, planting, transplanting, and harvesting machines.

To increase the area of agricultural land, North Korea launched a land reclamation scheme in the 1980s. One such scheme, completed in 1986, was the West Sea Barrage. The construction, which included the building of a 5 mile (8 km) dam across the Taedong River, cost $4 billion, and is believed to be the longest dam in the world. It provides the water for fish ponds and for farm and industrial use, and also generates electricity.

Fishing also plays an important role in North Korea, and the state has invested in "mother" ships and trawlers for deep-sea fishing in the waters of the Yellow Sea and the Sea of Japan.

Opposite top: **The West Sea Barrage blocks the flow of the Taedong River, creating an artificial lake that sends water through canals to irrigate agricultural land along the west coast of North Korea.**

Opposite bottom: **Village women sorting squid freshly caught on the coast.**

KOREA'S LEADING EXPORT: BABIES

During the 1980s, South Korea was the source of more than half of all foreign babies adopted in the United States. During that decade, more than 40,000 Korean babies became a part of American families. The number is dwindling in the 1990s because the South Korean government has drastically cut back on the number of babies released for foreign adoption.

Several conditions in the 1980s created the unique situation that has benefited so many American families. The first was the Korean War and a feeling of responsibility for the Amerasian children that resulted. Another is the fact that Koreans have traditionally shunned adoption because of their culture's strong emphasis on bloodlines and ancestry. Families take pride in keeping track of their ancestors in thick volumes of genealogical charts, leaving little room for children of different bloodlines.

But the situation is changing. Critics believe that South Korea, which wants to be viewed as a modern industrialized nation, should take care of its own people. Others believe that these Korean children should not be deprived of their cultural heritage. In 1990, the government announced that it wanted to shed its image as a baby exporter by reducing overseas adoptions by 10% to 20% each year and prohibiting them entirely by 1996.

The Ministry of Health and Welfare is hoping to encourage adoptions within the country by giving tax exemptions to families who adopt. A program has been established that places abandoned children temporarily with Korean families in the hope that the families will some day put these children's names on their *ho-juk* ("HOH-juck"), or family registers.

TRANSPORTATION

Korea's transportation system is growing rapidly. The highway system is well developed between major cities within each state. Both Seoul and Pyongyang also have a fine subway system. The bicycle is still a popular means of transportation in rural areas.

The state-owned rail system for both freight and passenger traffic has more than 4,000 miles (6,400 km) of track in South Korea, and another 5,300 miles (8,500 km) in North Korea. It is important in Korea's mountainous country, particularly in the north.

There are three international airports in Korea—at Seoul, Pusan, and Sunan, just outside Pyongyang. Korean Air and Asiana Air handle all domestic flights in South Korea as well as international flights. North Korea's national airline, Koryo, handles both domestic and international flights, the latter mainly to China and Russia.

THE KOREAN WORKER

Koreans have a strong work ethic. A recent survey revealed that the importance of work is second only to the family, and Koreans put in the hours to prove it. The average Korean in a manufacturing job works more than 55 hours a week, compared to the 40-hour week of the American factory worker.

Korean society is based on a deeply-rooted hierarchical social system. Koreans' respect for superiors takes the form of polite observances, such as rising in their presence and not leaving the work place before them.

The politeness and gentleness of Koreans lead foreigners to believe they are pushovers in business. Actually, they are highly competitive and tough negotiators. They are also fiercely loyal to individuals. A Korean would give a job to someone whose loyalty he values over a person who may seem more capable.

This modern subway station in Seoul also has an art gallery.

KOREANS

THE POPULATION OF KOREA IS NEARLY HOMOGENEOUS, meaning that nearly everyone in the peninsula is Korean. Typical Korean physical features include dark straight hair, straight noses, high cheekbones, and a single eyelid fold. The largest minority group are the Chinese, a scant 30,000 living in South Korea.

Koreans have great ethnic pride, and they strive to retain a single identity. Although there has been cultural contact between China and Korea throughout history, ethnic mixing was rare. Koreans have always been keenly aware of cultural and ethnic differences, and that allowed them to retain their homogeneity. The idea of multi-ethnic nations, such as the United States, is contrary to the Koreans' view of statehood. The Chinese of Korea are not even citizens; they are instead residents who fled China when the communist government took over that country in 1949.

Only since the Korean War has there been any racial mingling. During that time many American servicemen and Korean women married and started families.

45

SOCIAL SYSTEM

During the Yi dynasty, a hierarchical social system emerged that defined relations between people of different social levels. The classes were determined by occupation rather than by wealth. This social system also established an obligation to authority, resulting in a lack of individual rights. The four social classes were as follows:

YANGBAN The highest class, the *yangban* ("YAHNG-bahn"), were the power-elite. This class included the scholar-officials and military officials, and their families. Only the *yangban* could take the civil service examinations that measured knowledge of Confucian ideas. Passing the exams permitted them to hold positions in the government. If unemployed or poor, their status as *yangban* prohibited them from working, but they had to maintain the Confucian rituals and attitudes that made them figures of authority in their village.

CHUNGIN Between the *yangban* and the commoners were the *chungin* ("CHOON-in"). These individuals held positions as physicians, interpreters, craftsmen, artists, and military officers. *Chungin* served as important links between the common people and the *yangban*.

SANGMIN The *sangmin* ("SAHNG-min"), or commoners, made up about 75% of the population. This large class included farmers, merchants, fishermen, and minor administrators. The *sangmin* carried the burden of all taxation.

CHONMIN The lowest class was the *chonmin* ("CHOHN-min"), the "despised people." This group included slaves, servants, convicts, jailkeepers, shamans, actors, and female entertainers.

Above: **Today, village folk, usually farmers, often belong to the lower class because of their poverty.**

Opposite, top: **Farmers once belonged to the *sangmin* class.**

Opposite, bottom: **Craftsmen were from the more prestigious *chungin* class of Koreans who served as mediators between the *yangban* and the *sangmin*.**

Although these class distinctions were abolished in the 1890s, many descendants of the social elite living in the south still acknowledge their *yangban* roots. Class distinctions can influence marriage arrangements, political affiliations, and employment opportunities.

CONTEMPORARY SOCIAL CLASSES

Recently, a new class structure has emerged that is determined by wealth. Since the end of the Korean War, city dwellers in the south have grown richer because of industrialization and economic growth. These economically comfortable Koreans comprise the middle class that includes managers, healthcare professionals, and even factory workers.

The urban poor are decreasing and are mostly recent arrivals from rural areas. Koreans of the lower class generally live in rural areas, eking out a living by farming. Education is the key to social mobility.

DRESS

In the cities, most Koreans wear the modern Western fashions seen in London or New York. Older people, especially in rural areas, may still wear traditional clothing. Many old Koreans scorn modern fashion and take almost snobbish pride in wearing shabby, old-fashioned clothes. In the north, military uniform is present everywhere. During festivals, however, most Koreans don traditional dress when they take part in ritual celebrations.

The traditional Korean dress is called the *hanbok* ("HUN-bok"), which for men consists of bloomer-like pants called *baji* ("BAH-ji"), a short sleeveless jacket or vest, and a coat called a *turumagi* ("too-roo-mah-gi"). A woman's *hanbok* consists of a long, full skirt called a *chima* ("CHI-mah") and a short jacket or blouse called a *chogori* ("JUH-go-ri"). The *chogori* has a long sash that is tied in a bow on the side. The *hanbok* is typically white and is loose-fitting for cool comfort.

A *hanbok* is very comfortable, and can be worn in the home. For daily wear, the fabrics of choice are cotton and hemp. Silk, the fabric of royalty, is used on special occasions. Holiday clothing is marked by colorful stripes on the children's and women's sleeves.

It is not unusual to see rural *halmoni* ("HALH-muh-ni", grandmothers) and *haraboji* ("HAH-rah-buh-ji", grandfathers) in traditional clothes, looking as though they just stepped out of a photograph from years gone by. An old man will typically have dangling amber buttons on his jacket, rubber shoes with pointed, turned-up toes, and a tall hat called a *satkat* ("SUD-cut"), woven out of black horsehair. Underneath the hat, men often wear a long braid of hair, knotted on top of their heads.

Above: **Casual attire is the norm in Pyongyang, North Korea's capital.**

Left: **An old man wearing the traditional tall black hat and pointed rubber shoes.**

Opposite: **Two women in traditional dress, called *hanbok*. It consists of a long skirt and a short jacket, with a bow tied on the side.**

LIFESTYLE

THE BEHAVIOR AND THOUGHT of Koreans have been influenced by the philosophical and religious ideas that have entered Korea over the centuries. While economically modern, Koreans cling to many of the ways of their ancient ancestors.

All facets of Korean life, from housing to gender roles and education to friendship, have a Confucian slant, a slight Chinese influence, and a very identifiably Korean flavor.

CONFUCIANISM

Confucianism is not a religion, as some might believe. Based on the ideas of the Chinese philosopher Confucius, it is an ethical and social code of behavior, and the first organized way of thinking to be accepted in Korea.

Above: **Boys participating in a Confucian rite to honor the Chinese sage.**

Opposite: **Confucius, whose teachings greatly influence the Korean way of life.**

Confucianism does not involve the worship of any higher being; it is like some religions, however, in that it attempts to guide human relationships and improve conduct. As such, it is an all-encompassing philosophy on lifestyle. The fundamental thrust of Confucianism is to maintain peace and order. It has rules for relationships between family members and emphasizes harmony within these relationships. It stresses the importance of education and respect for authority.

The five most important relationships are between father and son, ruler and subject, husband and wife, elder and younger, and between friends. Koreans are very conscious of proper behavior and the loyalty of friends.

A family of three generations posing for a group photo in a park. It is common to see extended families enjoying leisure time together.

FAMILIES AND CLANS

The Korean family structure is part of a larger kinship system defined by specific obligations. The system consists of four levels: household, mourning group, lineage, and clan.

The first level in the Korean kinship structure is the household. The ideal Confucian family consists of four generations under one roof, but the urban family in Korea may not follow this pattern. Young married couples usually begin their lives together in an apartment away from their parents. In rural areas, however, it is still quite common to find a multi-generational household.

The traditional residence is made up of the husband and wife, their children, and the husband's parents if he is the eldest son. This arrangement is called the *jip* ("jip"), meaning the "big house." The households of younger sons are referred to as *chagunjip* ("CHAH-gehn-jip," little house).

In a Korean home, the head of the family (usually the oldest male) is the position of authority and each family member is expected to do as the family head says. There is an understanding, however, that the authority figure will always be fair in dealing with all those in the household. According to Confucian ideals, the authority figure also represents, supports, and protects the family. Should he not be able to tend to his family properly, he will lose face as the family head. Obedience to superiors—a totally Confucian concept—is what maintains order in the home and is a most admirable virtue. In the ideal Korean household, children obey their parents, the wife obeys her husband, younger brothers obey their older brothers, and so on.

The second level in the Korean kinship system is the mourning group or *tangnae* ("THANG-nay"), which is made up of people of the same ancestry going back four generations on their father's side. This group gets together at graveyards to participate in rites offering respect to ancestors.

P'a ("pah") is the third level of kinship and is the lineage that comprises all the descendants of one particular man. This group can be composed of thousands of households. It not only has responsibility for ancestral rites, but its members provide aid for needier members of the group and oversee the behavior of the younger members as well. A *p'a* often owns land and buildings that can be used by all the members, such as grave sites and schools.

A *tangnae* performing ancestral rites.

The highest level of the kinship system is the *tongjok* ("THONG-jok") or clan. *Tongjok* members have the same surname (family name), and because this group is so large, it generally does not have great feelings of solidarity. The most practical function of the *tongjok* is to determine the acceptability of marriage partners. There are strict rules against marrying someone who shares a common ancestor on the father's side, no matter how far back. By looking up a telephone directory, one can see that there are only about two hundred family names—and hence as many *tongjok*.

DEVOTION TO PARENTS

Filial piety is the sense of complete devotion of children to their parents. Korean children feel a great obligation to those who brought them into the world. The most intense of such observations of respect for one's elders is that between father and son. In Confucianism, this observance is even more important than the relationship between ruler and subject.

This deep dedication is considered an essential factor in the formation of one's personality. It is all part of the idea that the family, or group, is a more important unit in the framework of society than the individual. Filial piety is not aimed only at parents; it is a code of behavior that should be applied to all elders.

FRIENDSHIP

Loyalty between friends is also of tremendous importance to Koreans. This is one of the few relationships in Korean society that is based on equality. When two people become friends, it is a common expectation that they will remain friends throughout their lives.

Most friendships in Korea date back to schooldays, for that is a time in most Koreans' lives when peers are truly equals. Within the separate groups of males and females, no status markers differentiate students; each is involved in the same experience. Friends are expected to be there in times of need to

THE CLAN DILEMMA

South Korea remains the only country in the world where intra-clan marriages are banned. This causes tremendous difficulties for modern couples who decide to get married after falling in love before checking their family trees.

An estimated 300,000 South Korean couples are victims of this age-old ban, and as a result are involved in marriages that cannot be registered. Essentially, this means that these couples are not legally married. Men and women cannot claim tax exemptions for their spouses, and children of these unions are technically illegitimate. Some couples emigrate to give legal respectability to their marriage. Couples who cannot face the social pressures that result from these unauthorized nuptial ties separate because of the strain; some suicides have been reported.

The intra-clan marriage ban originated in China. Confucian scholars say that the ban was established in order to prevent the birth defects believed to result from the marriages of close relatives. To prevent improper matches, major clans still maintain offices and staffs that compile extensive genealogical records. In fact, the oldest recorded Korean ancestry, the Kimhae Kim clan, dates back to A.D. 42, nearly 2,000 years ago! While such impeccable record-keeping is admirable, it also serves to restrict young persons from following their hearts and marrying the person they truly love.

There is, however, much compassion for the plight of these people, even on the part of the government. Twice in the last 15 years the National Assembly declared a one-year suspension of the restriction on registering intra-clan marriages. During the first amnesty period, nearly 5,000 marriages became legal, and during the second, in 1988, more than 12,000 unions gained legitimacy.

China and North Korea have abolished their laws prohibiting intra-clan marriage, but two sections of South Korea's family law still ban such wedlock. Legal experts and feminists believe that an abolition of the ban is in South Korea's future. For a nation that wants to be seen as a modern country, the cancellation of this prejudicial law that focuses solely on the father's bloodline is probably just a matter of time.

lend support and to help solve problems. To deny a friend's request is unthinkable. As friends mature, their relationship extends from their personal lives to include their professional lives as well. Friends expect each other to provide contacts and opportunities throughout their careers. In 1987, for example, a great political debate centered around President Chun's intention, before he retired, to ensure that all the members of his graduating class of the Military Academy had suitable civil service posts so they would be taken care of in their military retirement years!

Opposite: **Boys having fun. Lifelong friendships cultivated during school days form "the old boys network" in their working years.**

Top: **A young woman worker in a South Korean printing plant.**

Bottom: **A train guard in North Korea.**

ROLE OF WOMEN

Korean society is male-dominated, and as a result the female role has always been a secondary and subservient one. Few women pursue careers, and the woman is actually thought of as the "inside" manager— the one who tends to matters inside the home. She is responsible for raising the children, handling the finances, and keeping the home running smoothly. If her husband's parents live with them, she must also serve them as obediently as she serves her husband.

In Korea, there were four groups of women who had more freedom throughout history. These were the shamans, or spirit mediums, who were hired to cure illnesses, communicate with ancestral spirits, and predict the future; female physicians, who were essential because males were not permitted to examine women; *haenyo* ("hay-NIO"), female divers; and *kisaeng* ("KEY-sang"), female entertainers. Although some *kisaeng* were prostitutes, others were talented musicians, poets, artists, and singers who were trained to provide lighthearted company for groups of men.

In modern South Korea, many young women work in export-oriented industries. In 1993, women accounted for 40% of the total workforce. Their contribution has been essential in the tremendous economic success of the nation because they work long hours for very low wages. These low-level jobs are usually held by young women and are abandoned once they get married.

Today, with more college-educated women, the number of working, professional women is increasing in fields like education, medicine, law, and business. Women in democratic South Korea are fighting for improved conditions by legal means, especially through the National Committee of Women's Policies and the Korean Women's Development Institute, both of which were created in 1983 through a presidential decree.

HAENYO—WOMEN OF THE SEA

In South Korea's traditional Confucian society, where one of the key principles is a woman's subservience to her husband, Cheju Island counters the norm.

On this island, just south of mainland Korea, women traditionally go out to work while the men stay home. These women are a dwindling group of robust females who dive year-round in the frigid waters off Cheju Island for sea urchins, abalone, and octopus. *Haenyo,* as they are called in Korean, carry on a tradition that goes back more than 1,500 years. It is a grueling, back-breaking vocation that has been passed down from mother to daughter. They do their deep-sea diving without any scuba equipment, for it is currently against the law to use such gear. They remain in the water for up to four hours a day in the summer and about 15 to 20 minutes in the winter, when the water temperature can plummet to about 50°F (10°C). Staying underwater for approximately three to five minutes at a time, they make shrieking noises as they release oxygen upon completion of a dive.

Before the invention of wet suits, *haenyo* were the natural choice as divers since women have more layers of fat beneath their skin than men do. Today, this traditional practice continues. These mermaids, who once ranged in age from 20 to 70 years, have long been the symbol of the island and the subject of folk songs, sculpture, and all manner of souvenirs.

While the *haenyo* appear to enjoy economic independence and greater autonomy than their mainland sisters, they are obliged to contribute one-fifth of their income to a fund that supports the many unemployed men of their villages. The rest of their money goes to husbands and sons, so that they can make the major financial decisions.

These women divers are a dwindling breed. In the 1970s there were about 24,000 divers, but now there are only a few hundred, all of whom are over the age of 50. Because it is a difficult and often debilitating job, modern women have chosen to break tradition rather than follow in their mothers' footsteps. The greatest difficulty for these divers is the effect of water pressure on their ears and sinuses. Many go deaf after years of diving and others become addicted to painkilling medications that they use to fight off discomfort.

Korean men and women may be modern in their dressing, but are conservative in their approach toward each other.

MALE-FEMALE RELATIONSHIPS

There is little intermingling between the sexes. Korean men and women have been segregated through the ages and still are today. There is little opportunity to develop social skills involving the opposite sex.

Men and women prefer to eat at different tables even at home, although this situation is changing when young couples are alone or do not live with parents. It is even rare to see men and women socializing freely at parties. This segregation of male and female roles has made it difficult for women to break into career fields that have long been considered "men's work."

Until recently, the relationship between husband and wife was not one of close friendship; rather it was based on the maintenance of obedient respect to the superior, the husband. As the modern Korean woman takes her place in society, however, the traditional relationships are slowly giving way to greater equality and friendship.

KIBUN

Kibun ("KEY-boon") is harmony. Maintaining harmony and good feeling is an all-important goal in interpersonal relationships in Korea.

Kibun can be ruined in several ways: by a person in a lesser position not showing the appropriate respect to a superior, by reprimanding a worker in the presence of others, by saying something negative about a person's hometown, or by simply handing something to a superior with the left hand, which is an etiquette blunder.

Koreans feel that preserving proper *kibun* is essential to accomplishment. If someone's feelings are hurt, or pride is lost in the course of reaching a long sought-after goal, the project is considered a failure.

Kibun is a very complicated process. In maintaining a harmonious and comfortable emotional atmosphere, an individual has to consider the state of mind of other people while keeping his or her own state of mind in a satisfactory condition. Judging the emotional demeanor of others is done through another Korean way of thinking called *nunchi* ("NOON-chi").

The wife's traditional relationship with her husband is based on obedience, not friendship.

NUNCHI

Nunchi is an intuition or "hunch" that helps a person "read" another person's state of mind. Those who can easily judge the body language, tone of voice, and general demeanor of people around them will find it easier to preserve *kibun* and social harmony.

A "human jam" at South Gate Market, Seoul. Crowded conditions like these are common in South Korea's large cities.

INTERACTIONS WITH STRANGERS

Foreigners who have visited Korea are often surprised to learn of the importance of *kibun*, for visitors always remark on the apparent disregard that Koreans have for strangers on the street. Koreans live quite comfortably in crowded conditions, as they do not have the same concept of personal space as Westerners do. Therefore the shoving and bumping that occur naturally appear as rudeness to foreigners who are accustomed to more space.

In addition to this, Koreans have no code of behavior toward outsiders. The Confucian system does not demand respect or loyalty to persons who have no connection with an individual. Once a Korean comes into contact with a particular person, he or she is no longer considered a stranger, and then all of the rules of respect and *kibun* are duly followed.

EDUCATION

As part of the Confucian heritage, education is highly valued by Koreans. Although education was traditionally reserved for people of the highest class, *yangban*, today it is available to all. As a result of universal education, Korea boasts a 95% literacy rate.

The education system, which is quite strict, has five levels in South Korea: a one- or two-year kindergarten, a six-year elementary school, a three-year middle school, a three-year high school, and a four- to six-year college or university program. In North Korea, there are four levels: one year of kindergarten, four years of elementary school, six years of middle school, and university. After finishing middle (or high) school, a student has several different educational options, including trade or industrial schools and evening classes in the south, and farming and industrial colleges in the north.

Education plays such an important role in the lives of the Koreans that the "right" education is the key to a good career and a secure future. A South Korean teenager typically studies long hours in preparation for the annual university entrance examination that will determine his or her future. Students prepare years ahead for the eight-hour examination that tests their knowledge in mathematics, history, English, chemistry, literature, and physics. The examination is the sole factor in determining whether a student will be admitted to most universities. When students fail, they must wait a full year before applying to another university and taking the examination again. Should they fail again, there is no third chance.

The tremendous competition creates "examination hell." Parents hire tutors for their children and totally change their lifestyle to offer moral and financial support throughout the final months before the examination. Sisters get factory jobs to bring in extra money so their brothers can hire tutors. Mothers wake early in the morning to help their children begin studying, and provide encouragement and nutritious meals long after midnight. According to the Ministry of Education, the pressure to excel academically is so great that in a recent six-month period as many as 51 high school students committed suicide because of their poor scholastic results.

A family playing *yut,* a traditional game, while sitting on their *ondol-*heated floor.

HOUSING

The traditional Korean home is a single-story structure that is usually L-shaped, U-shaped, or rectangular. Generally these homes are built of clay and wood with a thatched or tiled roof. But these typical houses can only be seen in rural areas today.

Newer buildings are made of concrete, and high-rise apartments abound in the cities to ease the housing shortage that has resulted from rapid urban growth since the Korean War.

Modern Korean houses are built with one main purpose: to keep out the cold. The rooms are small, and there are few doors and windows. Most houses have *ondol* ("ON-doll"), a domestic heating method that dates back to the Stone Age. *Ondol* is a system of air pipes, connected to the stove in the kitchen, that pass under the floor. As the warm air from the stove passes through the pipes, the floor becomes warm and comfortable to sit on.

Perhaps because of this heating method, most of the activities of a Korean family take place on the floor. Family members dine at a low table while sitting on the floor and sleep and sit on mats. Until recently there were few, if any, chairs or beds in a Korean home. With so much activity taking place on the floor, it is understandable that shoes are always removed before entering a Korean home.

LIFE CYCLE

BIRTH The Korean wife is put under tremendous pressure to produce a son to carry on the family bloodline. The preference for males is long-established in the patriarchal Confucian system, and the birth of a boy is considered a blessing.

Because it is of such importance, women offer prayers and follow rituals in the hope of having a baby boy. Offerings are made for 100 days to Taoist shrines, to Buddha, and to various natural entities such as rocks, trees, and astronomical wonders.

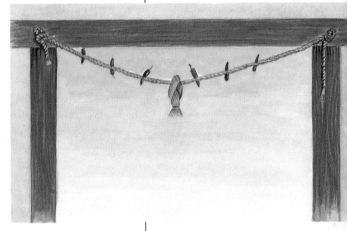

A line of chili peppers is hung across the doorway to frighten off evil spirits that may harm a newborn child.

The main spirit involved with childbirth is *Samshin Halmoni* ("SUM-shin Hul-MO-neh"), the grandmother spirit, because she provides for the child even after it is born, guiding its growth and well-being. Usually her shrine is inside the house, represented by a piece of folded paper or clean straw hung in a corner.

After the baby is born, there are many rituals to be followed. A straw rope of chili peppers, known as a *kumjul* ("KEHM-jool"), is hung across the gate or doorway of the house for three weeks to frighten evil spirits and warn people not to enter because a baby has just been born. Seaweed soup and rice are offered to the *Samshin Halmoni* every morning and evening for a week, and these foods are also eaten by the mother to speed up her recovery from the birth.

The newborn's family takes special care not to show their joy over the birth, because the spirits may become jealous and cause the baby harm. To mislead the spirits, beloved Korean babies are sometimes given unbecoming names such as Woodhead or Animal Dung!

A *tol* marks the child's survival during the crucial first year of life.

BIRTHDAY CELEBRATIONS In Korea, the first birthday, or *tol* ("DOUL"), and the 60th birthday, or *hwangap* ("HWUN-gup"), call for fanfare. And when a Korean baby reaches its 100th day, which in the past many failed to do, great rejoicing takes place.

The *paegil* ("PAY-gil") party, as the 100th-day celebration is called, is quite a jubilee. It marks the baby's survival of a critical period in infancy. Offerings of food are made to *Samshin Halmoni*, the grandmother spirit, and then family and friends celebrate with wine, rice cakes, and other delicacies. Only then are gifts presented to the baby.

Although the *tol*, or first birthday celebration, is enjoyed in much the same fashion, it is of even greater significance. Not only has the infant survived; if it is a boy, it is ready to choose its future career.

The pinnacle of the event comes when the baby boy, who is dressed in the finest *hanbok* (traditional clothing), is seated behind a small table where gifts and other items are placed. The child symbolically predicts his future by picking up an object from the table. If it is a piece of string or yarn, it is believed he will live a long life. If the choice is money or rice, a business career awaits. If he seeks cake or

BOY, WHERE ARE ALL THE GIRLS?

South Korea may be facing an unusual shortage: the number of girls born in the nation is steadily decreasing. As recently as 1980, 108 boys were born for every 100 girls; by 1988 the proportion had risen to 113 boys for every 100 girls. The worldwide average is 102.5 boys per 100 girls, therefore Korea's population of males is far greater than the norm. Have folk doctors in this male-dominated society found a way to conceive boys that Western doctors haven't yet discovered? Experts think not, but believe that medical technology is responsible for the growing imbalance.

Prenatal tests that reveal the sex of a fetus were introduced in South Korea in the early 1980s, just about the time the boy-girl birth ratio began to become distorted. Officials believe that pregnant women find out the sex of their child and abort the fetus if it is female.

Census figures of Taegu, a city in southeast Korea, seem to support this theory. Among families having a third child, nearly 400 boys are born for every 100 girls. For the fourth child born, the rate increased to 582 for every 100. Because most Koreans tend to have one or two children, it is common knowledge that people having more than two children are hoping for a boy; the two children they already have are almost certainly girls.

In the future, if the shortage of females becomes critical, parents will come to value daughters when their sons search in vain for a life partner.

"All Koreans go up one rank in prestige every year; they even start with a bonus—time in the womb counts as the first year of life, so that you are born at the age of one. Moreover, all birthdays occur on the Lunar New Year: if you are born in December, you are two almost before you can gurgle."

—*R.W. Howe, on Korean birthdays*

other food, a career in government service is in the offing, while the choice of a musical instrument will make him an artist. Guests leave the festivities with packages of rice cakes given by the child's parents, who believe that sharing these rice cakes will bring the child good health and happiness.

Hwangap, the 60th birthday, is celebrated because in the past few people survived until that age. Also, the Chinese lunar calendar used by the Koreans is based on 60-year cycles. Each year in the cycle has a different name, so when people reach their 60th year, the cycle returns to the year of their birth.

The family usually throws a lavish party, and loved ones gather to honor the celebrant. Rituals involve bowing to the celebrant and drinking wine, with traditional Korean music playing throughout the party. Rice cakes and fresh fruit are served as part of the feast, and a formal photograph is taken to commemorate the event.

A ritual in a wedding ceremony.

MARRIAGE Since being married is associated with maturity in Korea, few Koreans would choose not to marry. In fact, the Korean slang for spinster or bachelor is "big baby." The two types of marriage are love marriage or *yonae* ("yo-NAY") and arranged marriage or *chungmae* ("choong-MAY").

The Korean couple's first step in the *chungmae* is the meeting of the two families. The woman's parents probe into the man's character, his potential for success, and how the bride can expect to be treated. The man's parents set out to learn about the woman's character, health, and ability to fit into their family.

If this initial interaction goes well, the young people are left alone to get to know one another. If they do not get along, they will not be forced to marry. But if they are compatible, they go out on a few dates and discuss their expectations of married life. When everything seems in order, they return to their parents to announce that a marriage will be taking place.

Regardless of whether a young Korean couple is entering into a love marriage or an arranged marriage, one or both of their mothers will probably visit a fortune-teller who will read the couple's astrological charts to check for compatibility, and to determine an auspicious date for the wedding.

Short engagements of two to three months are usual, and in that short time both families must prepare gifts for each other.

THE WEDDING RITUAL

The bride's dowry is determined by the prestige of the groom's family. As a general rule, the bride must provide Western clothing for the groom's male relatives. Western clothing and traditional Korean dress must also be provided for the groom's female relatives. In addition, the bride often gives expensive jewelry to her mother-in-law.

The groom sends a *ham* ("HAHM"), a box of gifts for the bride, containing jewelry and fabric for a *hanbok*. A friend of the groom brings the box at a prearranged time, and when he gets within shouting distance of the bride's home, he shouts that he has a *ham* for sale. The family must coax the box from him with wine and food.

The traditional wedding ceremony is held in the bride's home. It begins with an exchange of bows and drinks. The bride and groom face one another across a table filled with objects symbolic of many aspects of the life they are about to begin together. This ceremony is followed by another called the *pyebaek* ("PAY-back"), which is the bride's first greeting to her husband's family. It is at this time that the bride presents the groom's family with their gifts.

After the ceremony, the wedding couple dresses in traditional wedding clothes for official photographs and to participate in bowing ceremonies to honor the marriage and the family.

The *chulssang,* or funeral procession, is a noisy affair that takes on the appearance of a festival.

OLD AGE Asians generally pride themselves on their care for the aged, and Koreans are no exception. With fewer extended families sharing homes, there has been a change in the way the elderly are cared for. Nonetheless, the elderly in Korea are still treated with great respect and children travel great distances each year to celebrate their parents' birthday. Strangers will give up their seats on buses and greet older people on the street with the appropriate honorifics or language showing respect.

Old age is a time for leisure. Many older Koreans spend their free time traveling in tour groups throughout the country to visit famous attractions that they have heard about all their lives but have never had a chance to see.

DEATH Korean customs and rituals surrounding death are also dictated by Confucian beliefs. Because of the emphasis on respect for parents and ancestors, careful attention is given to death rituals and funerals.

Dying at home is very important. Doctors try to provide ample notice to a family when a relative is critically ill, so they can transport the patient home before death. It is bad luck to bring a dead body into the home.

When someone dies, the body is covered with a white quilt, and formal wailing, known as *kok* ("kohk"), announces the death. The body is arranged so that it faces south, in a procedure called *chohon* ("CHOH-hon"). The next step is *yom* ("yohm"), the preparation of the corpse. This entails bathing the body in perfumed water and dressing it in ritual burial clothes.

Notice of the death is sent out, and those receiving it pay their respects at the home of the deceased. This visit to offer condolences is called *munsang* ("MOON-sahng"). Not conveying condolences is an offense to the grieving family and can create family feuds and end friendships.

The *chulssang* ("CHOOL-sahng") is the carrying of the coffin to the graveyard. This is accompanied by great fanfare, with some people carrying flags and incense, others carrying the coffin on their shoulders, and still others ringing bells and singing in a mournful voice.

Old men enjoying an afternoon in the park. For Koreans, old age is the time to enjoy life.

At the burial ground the family performs an ancestral ritual. There is occasionally some disagreement over which way is south, the direction in which the body should face. Once this has been sorted out, the oldest son throws the first handful of dirt on the coffin.

RELIGION

KOREANS ARE GRANTED freedom of worship in the Constitution, but this liberty is guaranteed only in South Korea. In North Korea, the Communist regime has repressed religion. Churches and temples were closed down and converted for other purposes shortly after the Korean War. The government of North Korea does not encourage religious practice for fear it will weaken Communist ideology.

While the majority of Koreans may say they are Christian or Buddhist, they mix the ideas and rituals of these religions with shamanism, which is deeply entrenched in the Korean way of life. For example, "God" in the Korean Bible is translated into *Hanamin*, a shaman word for "Great Spirit," and Buddhist temples are carved with shamanist deities.

SHAMANISM

Shamanism involves complex ceremonies to pay homage to the spirits of nature. In this earliest form of religion in Korea there is no focus on moral perfection or redemption. Shamanists believe that spirits or souls inhabit living and non-living things and that these souls can pass between humans, plants, rocks, animals, and other objects.

Shamans or *mudang* ("MOO-dung"), usually women, act as intermediaries between the human world and the spirit world. They are believed to be able to influence good and evil spirits. *Mudang* are especially interested in the souls of the dead and help resolve conflicts between the living and the dead. Ancient ceremonies such as the *kut* ("KOOD") are still held in Korea to cure illnesses by exorcising evil spirits, to gain a brighter future for a customer, and even to help guide a soul to heaven.

Above: **Spirit posts are erected to ward off evil spirits.**

Opposite: **A Buddhist priest chanting.**

71

AT YOUR SERVICE: THE *KUT*

A shaman's treatment is sometimes little more than family therapy. The first step in solving almost any problem, from domestic quarrels to financial difficulties, is to try to strengthen the relationship among family members and household gods. If the problem worsens instead, the diagnosis is that the gods want to play, or the family's ancestors are exerting a vengeful anger on family members. The solution for this is a *kut,* or shaman service.

The *kut* is a noisy ceremony with shouting and clanging of gongs. There are also songs, dances, and spell-chanting. The ceremony itself is a request to the gods or ancestors to enjoy the festive atmosphere, and thus dispel all ill-will.

At some point in the service, the *mudang* lapses into a trance and acts as the receptacle of the spirit. She speaks to the gods, who speak back through her. As things progress, all the women of the household and even the neighbors present begin to participate by shouting to the supernatural visitors. Vengeful ancestors who cause illness can be exorcised by tossing grain, whereas angry gods can only be appeased with offerings and treats.

Kut is often performed at the house of the person hiring the shaman, at the shaman's own home, or even outdoors, because the service itself must be adaptable to the type of problem it addresses. The ceremony often goes on all night, and as day breaks, the shaman and her aides beat drums and do a final exorcism for good luck.

BUDDHISM

Buddhism is one of the most popular religions in Korea, perhaps because Korean Buddhism is flexible and accepts shamanist deities. There are more than eight million Buddhists and nearly nine thousand Buddhist temples in the peninsula.

Buddhism came to the Korean peninsula during the Three Kingdoms period. The religion is based on the teachings of Siddhartha Gautama Sakyamuni, the Buddha, who was the prince of a small Indian kingdom in the sixth century B.C. The basic idea of Buddha's teachings is that salvation can come from giving up worldly desires and living in moderation. Living according to the Buddha's word can bring a person to the desirable state of Nirvana—ultimate peace wherein a person experiences no pain, worry, or worldly care.

Worship at a Buddhist temple.

Buddhism is divided into two main schools; the one practiced in Korea is the Mahayana school. This particular branch is tolerant of local spiritual practices and puts no restriction on reaching salvation. Because Buddhism has been a part of the religious fabric of Korea for so many years, it has mixed with some aspects of other religions. In fact, nearly every Korean Buddhist temple has a chapel next to it that contains a shrine to the mountain spirit. The mountain spirit's shrine receives the same respect that is bestowed on the Buddhist shrine. This practice ensures that the local mountain spirit, upon whose land the Buddhist temple sits, will not be angry.

There are nearly 30,000 churches in South Korea. There are about 2 million Catholics but one out of every six South Koreans is a Protestant.

TAOISM

Taoism came from China during the Three Kingdoms period and the teachings of Lao-tzu, its founder, still persist in Korea today. Because Taoism calls for the worship of many gods of equal importance, it is similar enough to shamanism for Koreans to accept easily.

Taoism's main focus is in creating harmony between man and nature. The many gods are used as ideals toward which humans can strive. Taoists believe that spiritual perfection can be attained in this life through simplicity, patience, purity, contentment, and harmony.

Although Taoism never became overwhelmingly popular in Korea, there are numerous traces of its influence throughout Korean society. The trigrams in each corner of the South Korean flag are taken from the *I-Ching*, the Chinese Book of Changes used by Taoist diviners of the future.

CHRISTIANITY

Christianity arrived in Korea in the 16th century, brought by Confucian intellectuals who learned about it in the Chinese capital of Peking (Beijing). Because new converts to Christianity refused to participate in ancestral rites, the government was firmly against Christian missionaries entering Korea to do their work.

The first half of the 19th century was a difficult time for Korean Christians: thousands were persecuted and many more were beheaded. Nonetheless, by 1865, there were more than 20,000 Catholics in Korea.

THE UNIFICATION CHURCH

One of the most controversial of South Korea's newer religions is the Unification Church, founded in Korea in 1954 by evangelist Sun Myung Moon, a former Presbyterian minister.

After World War II, Reverend Moon began teaching principles that were considered contrary to Presbyterian beliefs and he was expelled from the church in 1948. He started a new congregation, claiming to have once had a vision of Jesus Christ who gave him the mission of saving the world from Satan. These beliefs landed him in jail in North Korea, but he escaped two years later and fled to South Korea where he published his book, *The Divine Principle*. This work became the Bible of the Unification Church.

The stated goal of the Unification Church is to establish the rule of God on earth, an effort begun by Jesus Christ, but interrupted by Christ's crucifixion. Moon claims to have been entrusted by Jesus to complete the mission along with his wife, Hak Ja Han. Many of Moon's followers consider him to be the new Messiah.

No one knows the exact membership of the Unification Church; various estimates give figures ranging between 200,000 and 2 million worldwide. Members are often referred to as "Moonies," a name greatly disliked by the church. Some members live on communes and perform church-related work (usually fund-raising) or are employed by one of the many business enterprises owned by Moon. Critics of the Unification Church say that recruits are brainwashed and unable to exercise free will, are subject to strict discipline, and are urged to turn against their families.

Today there are more than 9 million Christians in South Korea, approximately 22% of its total population. This percentage is second only to the Philippines in East Asia.

Numerous denominations of Christianity are present, including Methodist and Presbyterian groups. Most of the Protestant denominations in Korea are fundamentalist. Protestant fundamentalism emphasizes the literal interpretation of the Bible as essential to Christian life. There are several minor Christian groups that some consider to be cult-like. A cult is generally described as a religious group devoted to a living leader or an unusual practice or teaching.

A throng entering an Evangelical church in South Korea.

Tolharubang, statues carved from basalt, are thought to be ancient village guardian deities.

NEW RELIGIONS

Modern religious movements in Korea are officially grouped by South Korea under the heading "new religions." There are nearly 250 of these, most of them having small memberships. They generally combine indigenous or native beliefs with Christianity.

The largest of the new religions is Chondogyo, the Heavenly Way, with a membership of approximately 600,000. This movement was founded in the 19th century by a scholar who had a vision that called upon him to lead mankind in the ways of heaven. Chondogyo was originally named Tonghak, which means "eastern learning," to differentiate it from Catholicism or Western learning. Chondogyo members' main belief is that all humans are equal and should be treated with respect because they have God within them. The religion is viewed more warmly by the Communist government of North Korea than other religions, since it is similar to some aspects of Communist ideology.

WAITING FOR THE RAPTURE

Among the many religious movements in South Korea, there is one that does not have much of a future, and its followers are thrilled! Members of the Mission for the Coming Days Church—about 20,000 strong—believe that the end of the world is coming and a phenomenon called the Rapture will lift the faithful to heaven.

The only problem is that they do not seem to have a clear idea of when this will happen. Church officials warned the membership that October 28, 1992 would be the day when white-robed angels would carry them to heaven, delivering them safely with trumpets blaring on their arrival. The only remaining evidence of their previous existence on earth would be their clothing, dental fillings, and church identification tags.

According to church officials, the Rapture would spark a seven-year war, resulting in flood, famine, and the eventual annihilation of Earth. This, in turn, would set the stage for a second coming of Christ.

Believers made preparations, some going so far as to sell property, abandon family and military obligations, quit jobs, and even commit suicide. As the day neared, church members spent up to 24 hours a day in one of the movement's 250 "churches," many of which were basements, offices, and abandoned warehouses with leases that expired on October 28. They spent their time praying to be among the ones taken to heaven. Plainclothes policemen monitored church activity.

South Korean officials were reluctant to meddle in the doomsday controversy because they did not want to infringe on religious freedom, which is guaranteed by the Constitution. Eventually the other churches issued appeals to quell the anxiety of the population.

When the day of the Rapture came and went without incident, church members remained steady in their faith, firm in their belief that their preparations would keep them in good faith for the next Rapture.

"Korean Christianity may conceivably be … a veneer, with Koreans fascinated by its mysticisms, such as the Trinity or the supernatural character of Jesus."

—R.W. Howe, on the nature of Korean Christianity

Another major new religion is Taejonggyo, which worships Tangun, the legendary founder of the Korean nation. That Taejonggyo is considered a new religion is ironic because it is actually Korea's oldest religion, dating back more than 4,000 years. It was considered a cult when it nearly disappeared in the 15th century, but in the last hundred years, several sects have arisen claiming to be a revival of this ancient faith. A few of the sects are very nationalistic and claim that Korea will be a world empire, and that a Korean will be the savior of mankind.

LANGUAGE

KOREAN IS THE OFFICIAL LANGUAGE and because of the vast number of people who speak it, it is considered one of the world's major languages. Most language experts agree that Korean originated in central Asia in the Altai Mountains. It bears some resemblance to other languages in the Altaic family (Turkish, Finnish, Mongolian, and the Manchu-Tungus languages) and is most like Japanese in general structure and vowel characteristics. The Korean writing system, known as *hangul*, is logical and practical, and possibly the single most important thing that ever happened in Korea because it brought literacy to the masses.

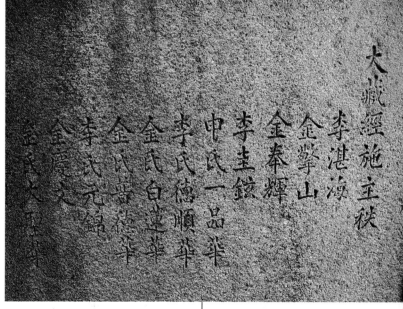

Above: **A rock carving of written Chinese, discovered in Pusan. The Chinese writing system was used in Korea until the creation of *hangul*, a phonetic system.**

Opposite: **Neon signs in Korean and English.**

There are regional Korean dialects, but these are similar except for a few words with slightly different pronunciation. Koreans from different regions of the peninsula can usually communicate with each other regardless of dialect, with the exception of the one spoken on Cheju Island. The official Korean dialect in South Korea is the one used in the region of its capital city of Seoul.

Korea's well-established social structure and its etiquette system call for different levels of language to appropriately distinguish between individuals and social classes. There are three language levels in use: a very polite form to address superiors, a personal form for speaking to equals or close friends, and a common or humble form for addressing people of a lower social level, or when referring to oneself.

Vowels Consonants	ㅏ [a]	ㅑ [ya]	ㅓ [ŏ]	ㅕ [yŏ]	ㅗ [o]	ㅛ [yo]	ㅜ [u]	ㅠ [yu]	ㅡ [ŭ]	ㅣ [i]
ㄱ [k,g]	가	갸	거	겨	고	교	구	규	그	기
ㄴ [n]	나	냐	너	녀	노	뇨	누	뉴	느	니
ㄷ [t,d]	다	댜	더	뎌	도	됴	두	듀	드	디
ㄹ [r,l]	라	랴	러	려	로	료	루	류	르	리
ㅁ [m]	마	먀	머	며	모	묘	무	뮤	므	미
ㅂ [p,b]	바	뱌	버	벼	보	뵤	부	뷰	브	비
ㅅ [s,sh]	사	샤	서	셔	소	쇼	수	슈	스	시
ㅇ	아	야	어	여	오	요	우	유	으	이
ㅈ [ch,j]	자	쟈	저	져	조	죠	주	쥬	즈	지
ㅊ [ch']	차	챠	처	쳐	초	쵸	추	츄	츠	치
ㅋ [k']	카	캬	커	켜	코	쿄	쿠	큐	크	키
ㅌ [t']	타	탸	터	텨	토	툐	투	튜	트	티
ㅍ [p']	파	퍄	퍼	펴	포	표	푸	퓨	프	피
ㅎ [h]	하	햐	허	혀	호	효	후	휴	흐	히

The consonants and vowels of *hangul*, the Korean alphabet.

HANGUL

King Sejong, who ruled the Choson kingdom from 1418 to 1450, was responsible for the creation of *hangul*. He wanted to enable all Korean people to write their language. In his day only the upper classes were educated and able to decipher the Chinese characters that represented the language of the Choson people.

King Sejong faced great opposition to this project because officials and scholars feared that Korean literature would be degraded—brought down to the "level of dust"—if it could be produced and understood by everyone. The king, however, persisted, for he understood the importance of literacy for all.

Hangul was first known as *hunmin chongum*, or the "right sounds for the instruction of the people." The main goal of King Sejong and the scholars he appointed was to devise a user-friendly alphabet system that closely represented the sounds of the Korean language as it was spoken then. It was a system designed to make it easy to learn to read and write.

Hangul uses a phonetic alphabet of 31 characters representing the sounds of the Korean language. There are 140 syllables in the alphabet, all combinations of 14 consonants, 10 vowels, and seven diphthong sounds. *Hangul* is easier to learn than many languages, including English. There are no capital letters, and vowels and consonants are easily differentiated.

In handwritten form, *hangul* looks like the squiggles of shorthand, but when rendered with a brush, in calligraphy, it looks like art.

VOCABULARY

As is the case with most modern languages, Korean is composed of both native words and borrowed words. Many English words have crept into the language; aspirin, supermarket, and bus are just a few examples. Scientific and technical terms make up the majority of borrowed Western words.

The greatest number of non-native Korean words come from Chinese, because Koreans have had contact with the Chinese for thousands of years. These words are often referred to as Sino-Korean words. Sino-Korean is to the Koreans what French is to the old aristocracies of Europe, a kind of elitist language.

Chinese numbers are generally used, especially after the number 10 and when counting items in successive order, such as in money and months.

STRUCTURE

Korean is an agglutinative language; in such a language, various affixes may be added to the stem of a word to add meaning or to show its grammatical function. Verbs are generally the last element in a sentence, while the other parts can be switched around freely.

A Korean street sign.

Like Japanese, Korean has no articles (a, an, the), and usually singular and plural forms are the same. In addition, the subject of a sentence is not used when it seems apparent. For example, "Are you going?" and "Are they going?" would be said in exactly the same way.

NAMES

Most Koreans have three names: a family name, which appears first, and two given names. The first given name identifies the person's generation and may be shared by brothers, sisters, and cousins. The other given name may be an attribute. Sons are sometimes given one of their father's own given names. For example, the late North Korean president, Kim Il Sung's son's name is Kim Jong Il.

Shamans, sages, or onomancers (official name-choosers) are often consulted before a Korean baby is named. Choosing the right name is considered instrumental in bringing good fortune to its bearer. Many parents name their children using positive characteristics, such as "wise" or "lovely," in the hope that the children will some day personify their names.

There are nearly 200 Korean surnames, but half the population are Park, Kim, or Lee. Other common family names are Shin, Han, Oh, Chang, and Choi.

A Korean woman does not change her family name when she marries. Although she may be called Mrs. Min in conversation because that is her husband's surname, she is really known by her birth name throughout her life. She may also be called *ojumoni* ("ah-JOO-moh-ni") or *puin* ("POO-in"), both of which mean "madam" or "aunty." Once she has a child, this title is dropped for another to indicate her new status; if her oldest child is named Sang-jun, for example, she would be known as Sang-jun's mother, even after Sang-jun's 50th birthday.

A rural woman playing with her child. Married women may be referred to as *ojumoni* or *puin*, meaning "aunty" or "wife," in a broad sense.

82

It is disrespectful to address the elderly by their given names. Generally speaking, the use of given names is restricted to a person's family members and friends whom he or she knows intimately.

TITLES

Titles are important, for it is impossible for a Korean to speak to someone in the correct manner if his or her status is unknown. Titles are necessary, too, because many people share the same surnames. In a large company where several persons may have the name Lee, the use of titles like Director Lee and Supervisor Lee avoids confusion. Titles may also impart information about birthplace, schools, and so on, so that the proper measure of respect is shown when speaking to a superior.

HONORIFICS

Honorifics are forms of polite speech worked into a language that play a significant role, especially when addressing an older person or one of a higher social class. Suffixes to show respect, for example, *"an-nung-ha-sin-ni-ka"* ("AHN-nyong-HAH-shin-NI-kah"), a blessing of peace and good health, should end any discourse with an elder.

Honorifics may also be used to flatter someone. A Korean may address another as *Yangban* (ancient title of nobility), just as a Westerner may address another as Boss. The title *Paksa* ("PAK-sah"), for teacher, may be used to address someone who has been offended, in the hope he or she will assume the self-restraint expected of teachers, and not be justly angry.

A very polite form of address is always used when speaking to the elderly.

This special bow, called *se-bae* ("SAY-bay"), is performed on special occasions; in this case it is a wedding ritual. Both palms are on the floor and the head is lowered all the way to the ground.

NONVERBAL COMMUNICATION

Nonverbal communication is a universal aspect of human behavior. Certain involuntary physical actions such as smiling, laughing, and crying are behaviors known throughout the world, whereas many others are culture-bound.

BOWING In Korea bowing is performed at various times throughout the day to symbolize different things. Koreans bow when they meet. The person of lower status bows first and says a greeting, then the other quickly bows and responds in kind. If the person being greeted is of much higher status (a father receiving a greeting from his son, for example), he may not bow, instead expressing an intimate greeting.

Koreans also bow when being introduced for the first time, and they bow when they part. There are degrees to bows, ranging from a quick dip to a 90° bow that shows great respect. The greatest degree of respect requires the bower to lower the head all the way to the ground while touching both palms to the floor. This gesture is used in temples or in homes—not in the office or on the street. Much can be told by the way two Koreans greet one another—the teacher, doctor, and grandfather are easily distinguished from the student, patient, and grandson.

GESTURES Many people wrongly assume that gestures have a universal meaning. Korean gestures can be quite different from American ones. For example, the wave that an American would understand as "goodbye" would actually mean "come" to the Korean. To wave goodbye, Koreans wave their lifted forearm side to side, palm facing out. The American gesture of "come," with the palm facing upward is used by Koreans only to call a dog. The way to induce someone to come closer is to extend the arm with the palm downward, making a scratching motion.

Koreans always use the right hand when handing an object to a superior. To show greater respect, the left palm will support the right elbow. The utmost respect is shown by handing an object to a superior with both hands. Use of the right hand is so associated with respect that children showing a tendency toward left-handedness are encouraged to acquire right-handed behaviors.

It is impolite to maintain eye contact for a long time, so Koreans often look to either side during a conversation.

EYE CONTACT AND FACIAL EXPRESSION Unlike Westerners, who try to maintain eye contact throughout a conversation, Koreans maintain eye contact only part of the time. When they are not looking into the eyes of the person they are conversing with, they look to either side, but not up or down. Those of higher status maintain longer eye contact than people of lower status. Only when arguing or transacting business will Koreans keep long eye contact. When being scolded, a Korean will look down slightly. The eye contact rule does not apply to strangers, however. Koreans will stare at people at a bus-stop if they are curious about them, a behavior that disconcerts foreigners.

While Koreans smile when they are happy, they also smile when they are ashamed or uncomfortable. A person who displeases a superior may smile for an entire day, which presents a very perplexing sight for the uninformed foreign observer. When laughing, Korean women often cover their mouths.

ARTS

KOREAN ART HAS been largely influenced by Japan and China. Regardless of the many shared characteristics in the arts of these three countries, Korean art has developed its own distinctive style. Themes are usually centered around love for nature, loyalty to the king, and admiration for learning. The art forms that have been developed most fully include music, dance, poetry, pottery, sculpture, and painting.

The Korean dynasties that ruled the peninsula from A.D. 668 through the first few years of the 20th century encouraged the arts. Dancers and musicians were always an integral part of the court. But most of Korea's notable advancement in the arts came during the Unified Silla period (A.D. 668–917), when Buddhism also had a profound effect on the arts and scholarship.

Above: **A performance of** ***sogak*** **or "music for the people."**

Opposite: **A carved and painted temple roof. Temple art in Korea is highly developed. It is similar to Chinese temple art as Chinese influence was strong for a very long time.**

Countless temples, pagodas, and palaces were built, and the production of painting, ceramics, lacquerware, and jewelry flourished. Little is known of the artists, however, because the work was usually executed by slaves on the orders of the aristocracy, it would have been improper for a slave to put his seal, or chop, on the work.

The Japanese occupation of Korea, from 1910 through the end of World War II, impeded Korean cultural pursuits. Cultural advancement in South Korea since 1948 has been rapid and remarkable, with equal focus on traditional forms and new innovations. Traditional fine arts are also strongly encouraged by the North Korean government because an appreciation of these promotes nationalism. Artists and writers are assigned to government institutions such as the National Theater for the Arts, the National Orchestra, and the National Dancing Theater.

PANSORI

Korean narrative opera, known as *pansori* ("PAHN-soh-ri"), is an art form that captures the very character and culture of Korea by teaching traditional virtues through a story. An example of a *pansori* is the popular story of a young woman who withstands persecution to remain faithful to a noble admirer. The story touches on all the important Korean qualities: loyalty, brotherly love, friendship, and respect for parents.

In *pansori*, a single performer beats out rhythms on a drum while vocalizing all of the roles and reciting the narrative between the songs. Although it is a one-man show, the performer appears to have a dialogue with the audience. A complete *pansori* can last up to six hours.

Korea's best known *pansori* performer is 82-year-old Kim Myong Hwan, who, in 1978, was declared a living national treasure by the government.

While always considered a vital Korean art form, *pansori* has recently experienced a revival among students, some of whom have embraced it as a form of rebellion against Western art forms. Other students draw on the techniques of this traditional drama to satirize the contemporary political scene.

MUSIC

There are two types of traditional Korean music: *chongak* ("CHONG-gak"), music for the noble people, and *sogak* ("SOH-gak"), music for the common people. *Chongak* includes Confucian ritual music, court music, and secular music of Chinese origin. *Sogak* includes shaman music, Buddhist music, folk songs, farmer's music, operatic ballads (*pansori*), and instrumental solo music (*sanjo,* "SAN-joh").

Folk music varies from region to region, but common to all are the Buddhist and shamanist elements.

The music of farmers' dances is probably the oldest known folk music, having been handed down from generation to generation since the ancient Three Kingdoms period. The original intention of this folk music was to appease the nature spirits, but eventually it became more of an amusement for people than a perceived influence on the supernatural world. Nonetheless, some still consider folk music to have a positive effect on the spirits; therefore, farmers' dances and music are still performed to ensure good crops, purify a village's drinking water, and protect houses.

Above: **Court music being played by musicians in traditional dress.**

Opposite: **Women playing the popular** *kayagum* **("KAH-yah-gehm"), a 12-string zither that originated in southern Korea.**

A court dance being performed with elaborate costumes but simple steps.

DANCE

Traditional dances in Korea have always been of great interest to the Korean public. That they probably developed from shamanistic rituals more than 3,000 years ago is evident by the fact that these dances are closely associated with agricultural cycles.

Korean dances differ greatly from most Western dances in at least one aspect: there is no choreography, for these dances are supposed to be spontaneous and improvisational. A Korean dance does not tell a story; instead it conveys feelings and evokes emotions. Two key elements are involved, *hung* ("hahn") and *mot* ("mot"). *Hung* is a state of mind, an inner feeling or mood; *mot* is grace and spiritual inspiration. To achieve *hung* and *mot* depends more on inner resources than on adherence to dance techniques.

In Korean dances, the arms and upper torso play a much greater role than the feet, which are often hidden beneath billowing skirts. Poses are seldom struck; instead there is a fluidity to the motion, and that, combined with airy costumes, gives the impression that the dancers are floating rather than performing steps.

Korean dances have three forms: court, religious, and folk. Court dances are performed by both male dancers and *kisaeng* (female entertainers). In the past, this type of entertainment was produced only for a royal audience. The costumes worn are quite elaborate in contrast to the steps, which are simple. There are two types of court dancing, one of Korean origin and the other of Chinese origin. The most popular court dance is called *Hwaganmu* ("HWA-kwan-moo"), or Flower Crown Dance, named for the flowered crowns worn by the dancers.

The best-known of the religious dances are the shamanistic dances performed to invoke the spirits that send the *mudang,* or shaman, into a trance. Others in the religious category are Confucian dances—stiff, cere-monial forms that were first performed in China. Confucian dances are still performed in spring and fall during ceremonies at shrines.

Mask dances originated during the Yi dynasty (1392–1910). The quality of a mask dance lies in the skill of the actor: the livelier the actor, the more animated the dance.

Folk dances are the most representative of Korean dances. The farmers' dances are the oldest surviving dances in Korea. In these dances, performers spin wildly to the beat of drums and gongs. Folk dances are still performed to purify homes, invoke good spirits, and drive out evil ones.

Perhaps most distinctive of all Korean folk dances are the mask dances. These originally served as a means for people to express their anger and disappointment toward the government and clergy. The themes of these dance dramas are corruption, greed, hypocrisy, stupidity, and fraud. The masks are the focus of the satirical dramas; drums, cymbals, and flutes provide the musical accompaniment. The masks are burned after each performance, for it is thought that the spirits contaminate them.

LITERATURE

Classical Korean literature focuses almost exclusively on history and on nature. Prior to the 20th century, almost all the literature of Korea was written in Chinese, for *hangul*, the alphabet created for all Koreans, was despised by many scholars.

Some of Korea's best-known literary works are the *History of the Three Kingdoms*, which was written in the 12th century, and *Memorabilia of the Three Kingdoms*, from the 13th century. Not only do these works serve as major literary achievements, but they provide almost all known information on ancient Korean history.

Korean poetry dates back to the 6th century. Short lyrical poems called *hyangga* ("HYUNG-gah"), 6–12 lines long, were written during the Silla dynasty, using Chinese characters. After the advent of *hangul,* a characteristic poetic form, known as *sijo*, grew in popularity. *Sijo* is a very short ode, sometimes only three lines long. As people became more proficient in writing *hangul,* they found that the short *sijo* could not convey their very complex emotions, so they began expressing their thoughts in the lengthier *kasa* ("KAH-sah") verse. *Sijo* and *kasa* are considered among the most characteristic forms of Korean poetry because they were not recited, but written and sung by all Koreans.

Novels also appeared after *hangul* came into use. Two of the most famous early novels are *Dream of the Nine Clouds* and *Tale of Lady Sa*. Many early novels were also written about military experiences. The period from 1725

SIJO

Alas, what have I done?
    Didn't I know how I would yearn?
Had I but bid him stay,
    how could he have gone? But stubborn
I sent him away,
    and now such longing learn!

—*Translated by David R. McCann*

This verse was composed by Hwang Chi-ni, a famous *kisaeng* from the Three Kingdoms period who wrote *sijo* poetry. *Kisaeng* were women who entertained men with music and dance.

through 1800 is considered the time when traditional Korean fiction really came of age.

Modern literature in Korea, focusing on social and political issues, began to develop in the 20th century. The historical novel remains popular among readers and writers.

PAINTING

Korean painting was influenced by Chinese art. Chinese-style wall paintings that date back to A.D. 400 were discovered in tombs in Koguryo (present-day North Korea). These works are brightly colored and depict the peoples and lifestyles of Korea around the time of Christ. During the Choson or Yi dynasty, Korean painting developed its own unique and natural form. Distinctive styles of composition and treatment of space emerged, as did brush-stroke techniques.

Women being taught the basics of Korean painting. The paintings in the background focus on nature scenes.

Korean folk painting was overlooked for centuries because it was produced by the less educated classes. Confucian scholars spurned the colorful works of the common people because they did not reflect the "correct" religious and intellectual values. It was customary to destroy or bury old paintings when new ones were created, therefore much old folk painting will never be recovered.

Minhwa ("MIN-hoo-wa"), as these folk paintings are called, provide a real view of everyday life. The main theme of *minhwa* is humans' relationship with their environment—a theme that is expressed in Buddhism, Taoism, shamanism, and Confucianism. *Minhwa* is seen as a true indigenous artistic expression of the Korean people.

CALLIGRAPHY

Calligraphy, which literally means beautiful writing, is an art form that is more highly regarded than painting in Korea, China, and Japan. Throughout history, calligraphy has had a strong influence on Korean culture. It remains a respected art form and is taught in schools of calligraphy by masters of the art.

Calligraphy is the composition of a few characters in an aesthetically pleasing manner. Although *hangul*, the Korean writing system, was invented in the mid-1400s, Chinese continued to be used as the official script until the late 1800s.

As Confucianism and its focus on the importance of education developed throughout the Choson period, calligraphy became a cherished skill. Among the nobility, the only class that knew how to write, calligraphy was considered an essential discipline for a refined gentleman.

Truly artistic calligraphy depends on the creativity and talent of the writer to give interesting shapes to the strokes of the written characters. Each stroke must be perfect; there is no retouching or shading. The strokes must be balanced, a skill that the artist acquires only after years of practice. Communication is not the main thrust of calligraphic writing; rather it is seen as a whole composition, admired as a well-executed piece of art. This exquisite, stylized writing is considered an art form closely related to painting, and is hung on walls, as a painting would be.

SCULPTURE

Archeological diggings have revealed clay, bone, and stone figures of animals and man from Neolithic times, but it is believed that sculpture really began to develop after Buddhism was introduced to the Korean peninsula, around A.D. 500. A classic piece of sculpture from this period is a gilt-bronze standing image of Buddha that was discovered in 1967. An inscription on it corresponds to the year A.D. 537.

Some of the most remarkable accomplishments in stone art sculpture are found in the Sokkuram Grotto Shrine, dating to A.D. 900. The shrine has 37 stone images considered to be among the most beautiful Korean sculptures.

Pagodas and stupas, which are cylindrical Buddhist shrine mounds, are also considered typical of Korean sculptural art. Most are decorated with Buddhist images and religious designs.

Modern sculpture in Korea began to gain popularity in the 1960s. Realism and abstract ideas were more greatly appreciated, and an increasing number of materials were used. Two major movements emerged. One, known as the "anti-formal abstract movement," became quite popular, as sculptors freely expressed their emotions through unconventional, abstract shapes. Then the "sculptural conceptualism movement" evolved, producing simple forms. Current sculptural trends are taking on a more nostalgic, humane nature.

CRAFTS

METALCRAFT A great number of relics of ancient ages have been uncovered in Korea. Relics of the Bronze Age, including mirrors, knives, bells, belt hooks, and ornamental ritual ware have been found all over the peninsula. Metalcraft was a refined art in Korea by 100 B.C. One of the truly exceptional Korean metalcraft products is bells. Only a few, dating back to the Silla dynasty (A.D. 668–917), remain today, and their artistic merit has been acknowledged throughout the world.

POTTERY Perhaps the best-known of Korea's art objects is pottery. Almost every museum in the Western world has some Korean celadon pottery. Celadon was first produced in Korea in about A.D. 1050, when artisans discovered a way to inlay design on pottery, which was glazed and fired at an extremely high temperature. The method produced pieces in a watery blue-green color that are now famous. Celadon pottery has a range of different colors.

The **Emillie Bell** is 1,000 years old and weighs 20 tons. It is the largest bell in Korea. When struck, it can be heard 40 miles (65 km) away.

LEISURE

KOREANS HAVE one of the longest work weeks in the world, leaving them little time for leisure. But the same intense attitude they apply to work is brought to their leisure, whether it be sports, nightlife, television soaps, or video games. North Koreans lead a more austere existence than their southern cousins, with regimented leisure activities like organized museum tours, but they too enjoy vigorous games.

Hostility between north and south has occasionally tarnished sportsmanship. Unfortunate incidents, such as North Korea's boycott of the 1988 Olympics in Seoul, have occurred. Yet, in 1991, the two nations sent combined table tennis teams to Japan, and emerged champions. To Koreans anxious for reunification, it seemed to be a good omen.

Above: **Taking a break from their military duties, these young North Koreans enjoy a game of volleyball.**

Opposite: ***Ssirum*** **is a traditional sport similar to Japanese sumo wrestling.**

SPORTS

The popularity of sports in Korea has increased steadily. Koreans are highly competitive and health-conscious. They consider athletic activity essential to their development, and involve their children in physical competition very early in life.

SOCCER International sports have slowly made their way into Korea. Soccer, the most popular, was brought to Korea in 1882 by sailors on a merchant ship. The South Korean soccer team is a premier player in the Asian Games, an Olympic-type athletic competition held every four years. In 1986, the South Korean team captured the gold medal in soccer.

SETTING RECORDS

The Korean Guinness Association is an organization established in 1989 for the sole purpose of setting records that would be recognized by the Guinness Book of World Records. South Korea thinks that in spite of its recent economic success, the rest of the developed world does not give it the respect it deserves. One way to gain that respect and improve the country's image, some South Koreans believe, is by establishing all sorts of world records.

The association has more than 3,000 members who pay $50 yearly to support the organization's activities. From the membership, a team of certifiers has been organized to travel from village to village looking for remarkable feats and accomplishments. In its first year of operation, the association managed to establish 19 very diverse world records, ranging from a tiny village of 275 families with 38 sets of twins to the world's largest chandelier, found in the Lotte World Hotel.

South Korea's appetite for world records was whetted when it hosted the 1988 Summer Olympics in Seoul. The event unwittingly set records for the most competitors in an Olympics, the most nations competing, and the largest drum in the world, which was used in the opening ceremony. It was then that the dream of setting records was launched.

To help in the process of establishing world records, the head of the association hosts competitions where people are invited to set records. Exciting though the quest for records may be, it is not always easy. The Korean Guinness Association has found that the London-based Guinness organization can be hard to please. Rules must be carefully followed, feats cannot be unnecessarily dangerous, and all accomplishments must be able to be measured and compared. After submitting certified events, the Korean Guinness Association must wait to hear whether or not the London organization accepts the record. One decision the Korean organization anxiously awaited was the record of a man who supposedly wrote 243 Chinese characters on a rice grain!

The goal of the Korean Guinness Association is to some day have more world records than the United States, which has nearly 300. But a more immediate and very satisfying aim is to beat its arch rival, Japan, which has about 50 Guinness records.

BASEBALL High school baseball games draw great crowds, and the nationwide high school tournaments are big events. South Korea's ability to compete on an international level was shown when it captured the World Little League title in 1984. In the 1980s, a professional baseball league was established, providing much spectator excitement.

VOLLEYBALL Another 20th century import to Korea, volleyball is enjoyed by men and women alike, with both groups competing quite successfully in the Asian Games. The advancing skills of the Korean teams has induced other nations to recruit Korean volleyball coaches for their teams.

TABLE TENNIS As it is in most of Asia, table tennis is a popular sport in Korea. During the 1986 Asian Games, the South Korean teams beat the much-feared Chinese teams in three of the seven table tennis events. In 1979, North Korea prevented the South Korean team from competing in the world table tennis championships by not issuing visas to the Seoul team to compete in the North. Since then, there has been some cooperation between the two Koreas, resulting in the peninsula's victory in the 1991 world championship title that was held in Japan.

ARCHERY Archery is one of Korea's oldest sports, one in which noblewomen could participate without fear of criticism. The South Korean women's archery team has made a very impressive showing in the Olympic Games, taking the gold in both the 1988 and 1992 Summer Olympics.

OTHER SPORTS Other sports that are played and enjoyed in Korea include golf, boxing, tennis, rifle-shooting, and skiing.

Korean female athletes excel in archery, traditionally one of the only sports women were allowed to participate in.

99

TAEKWONDO AND SSIRUM Two sports that are traditionally Korean are *taekwondo* ("tay-KWAHN-doh") and *ssirum* ("SEE-rehm"). Taekwondo is a self-defense martial art that originated in Korea more than 2,000 years ago. It is practiced by nearly every able-bodied Korean man at some time in his life and is considered the Korean national sport. This Korean martial art has become very popular throughout the world, and Korean instructors are employed in more than 100 countries to teach the sport.

Ssirum, meaning "the competition of man," is a Korean form of wrestling similar to Japanese sumo wrestling. It is believed to be more than 1,500 years old and was originally a means of self-defense. Over the years it has become a sport. *Ssirum* has very simple rules, and it is a favorite among farmers and fishermen. This native form of wrestling is also taught widely in Korean middle and high schools.

Taekwondo originated in Korea about 2,000 years ago.

TRADITIONAL PASTIMES AND GAMES

Korea's traditional games were developed over the centuries. Many of them have their roots in China, and few are truly Korean. Because Korea was such a poor nation for so many years, many of their games require very little equipment. It is customary to play these games during festivals.

PAENGIL *Paengil* ("PHAENG-yi") is top-spinning. Children keep their wooden tops spinning by snapping a string at the pointed bottom of the

top. The string is attached to a stick, giving the appearance of children fiercely whipping at a tiny object on the ground. In the winter children often play *paengil* on ice.

TAK SSAUUM *Tak ssaum* ("TAK-saom") is a child's version of cock-fighting. Children hold one foot up with their hands and then try to knock their opponents down while hopping around.

PADUK *Paduk* ("PAH-dook") is a traditional adults' activity that uses a board with a grid pattern of 19 vertical and 19 horizontal lines. Black and white stones are used to try to gain and keep control of an area, while attempting to capture the opponent's stones in the process. It is a game of strategy and is often a battle of wits. Most Koreans know how to play *paduk*, and *paduk* professionals play in international tournaments.

CHAJON-NORI *Chajon-nori* ("CHAH-john-NOH-ri") is a powerful battle in which two sets of poles are placed so that their tops meet. Near the top of each set a man fights to knock his competitor off. Other men hold the poles at the bottom and try to steer their team-mates to victory.

Women playing *noldwigi*, a traditional seesaw activity.

CHANGGI This Korean-style chess game is played on a board. Like chess, the game symbolically represents war, and each player has 16 pieces to maneuver. In the case of *changgi* ("CHANG-gi"), the object is to capture the general. A younger or amateur player is always allowed to make the first move.

NOLDWIGI *Noldwigi* ("NOL-di-gi") is a Korean seesaw activity enjoyed mostly by adult women. A long board is balanced on a bag of rice straw or a rolled-up straw mat. The women stand on each end of the board and one jumps forcefully on it, so that when she lands she sends the woman on the other end as high as possible. Similar to the custom of swinging, this was a way for isolated women to catch a glimpse of the world outside the high fence surrounding their yard.

KITE-FLYING Kite-flying has long been a favorite of Koreans, both young and old. Kites, or *yon* ("YAWN"), are almost always rectangular, made with bamboo ribs, paper, and glue. They have a round hole in the center and

are decorated with geometric designs. A popular time for kite-flying is during the Lunar New Year. On the last day of the new moon, people traditionally let the kite go, hoping that bad luck will float away with it!

YUT *Yut* ("yoot") is usually played on Lunar New Year's Day. Originally a divining game to predict future events, *yut* is believed to have been brought to Korea by the Mongols. In this game four sticks, flat on one side and rounded on the other, are thrown into the air. Points are given for the side on which the sticks land. The team with the most points in each turn advances around a circle. The winning team is the first to finish.

TUG-OF-WAR This is a traditional game in which entire villages or counties compete against one another. Each team makes a straw rope of an agreed length and thickness. The ropes are knotted together when the competition begins. The team pulling one of the ropes is considered the female side, whereas the other is the male side. When the female side wins, everyone is happy for they believe it symbolizes a good harvest.

Yut **is played on Lunar New Year. A good portion of the fun comes from the yelling and cheering by spectators. Sometimes food and drink accompany the activity, and sometimes gambling on the outcome adds excitement.**

FESTIVALS

TWO KINDS OF HOLIDAY are celebrated in Korea: traditional/cultural/religious-based holidays and political/historical holidays. Almost all the holidays in North Korea are political anniversaries. These, like South Korea's Constitution Day, have only been part of the Korean scene for a few decades. A calendar of holidays of both nations is given at the end of this chapter.

Because Korea was an agricultural society for many centuries, festivals were agriculturally based. The lunar calendar was most useful in agriculture because certain days based on the phase and positioning of the moon were optimal for planting. Other days were designated to celebrate the harvest. No matter what the historical event, season, activity, or religious significance, the Koreans celebrate their holidays with gusto.

Left: **The drum is usually present when a Korean festival is celebrated.**

Opposite: **Lotus flower lanterns assembled outside a temple in preparation for the festivities of Buddha's birthday.**

A formal bow on New Year's Day.

NEW YEAR

The New Year is a major occasion in Korea, and it occurs twice a year in the south! The first two days of January are designated as national holidays in North Korea; for South Korea it is January 1-3. In the south, the first three days of the Lunar New Year, called *Sol-nal* ("SUHL-nahl," the first day of the first moon in the lunar year) are also holidays. Although it has been observed for centuries, *Sol-nal* only became a legal holiday in South Korea in 1985.

Often only rural folk celebrate the New Year on *Sol-nal*, while city people celebrate it on January 1. Some people celebrate both. Regardless of which date is chosen, great preparations must be made for the New Year. Old debts are often repaid, and houses are made immaculate. The focus of this holiday is honoring one's elders and ancestors. Children in new *hanbok*, a new pair of shoes, and new socks make a formal bow to their elders. Parents and grandparents generally give blessings, money, or other small gifts to the children. Greeting cards and simple handmade gifts are exchanged.

Family gatherings and visits to friends are also an important part of this holiday. Cousins, aunts, uncles—all the members of the extended family— come together in the home of the eldest person for a memorial service to their dead ancestors, a Buddhist tradition. Food is prepared and set in front of photographs of the departed ones. Deep bowing takes place, first in front of the ancestors, then in front of the eldest living relatives. The following days are devoted to visiting persons to whom respect is due. For example, employees visit their bosses; students, their teachers.

TAE-BO-RUM (THE GREAT MOON FESTIVAL)

Tae-bo-rum ("TAY-boh-rehm"), or the first full moon, is celebrated on the 15th day of the first lunar month. In the past, the Korean New Year festivities ended on *Tae-bo-rum.*

During *Tae-bo-rum,* fire signals the momentous sighting of the first full moon in the lunar year.

The moon has always been an object of fascination and adoration for Koreans. Farmers used to think they could predict the weather for the coming months by the color of this first full moon—a golden moon foretold perfect weather, a reddish moon meant little rain.

Because catching a glimpse of the first full moon as it rises is thought to bring good luck for the coming year, everyone gathers in the afternoon, often on a hilltop, to see the rim of the rising moon. Those in the countryside light little mounds of twigs to signal the momentous event.

It is a very cheerful and rousing time. Neighboring villages engage in tug-of-war competitions, mock torch fights, and stone fights. Youngsters spend the day searching for good luck charms and doing things nine times for good luck.

Special *Tae-bo-rum* foods include peanuts, chestnuts, and walnuts, for Koreans believe that these foods will give them clear skin for the rest of the year! Another dish called *o-gok-pap* ("OH-gohk-pahp"), made of five grains, is a traditional offering during this festival.

Pink-flowering cherry trees mark the beginning of spring.

CHERRY BLOSSOM FESTIVAL

When the cherry trees bloom in Korea in early April, the air is filled with a sweet scent and beautiful pink-blossomed trees line the streets. So lovely are the trees in bloom that Koreans take their children on day-long trips just to enjoy their beauty during the Cherry Blossom Festival.

The Japanese planted the first cherry trees in Chinhae, where they established their naval headquarters in Korea during the Japanese colonial period (1910–1945).

At the end of World War II, when the Japanese surrendered and the South Koreans gained their independence, most of the cherry trees planted by the much-disliked Japanese were uprooted. Since then, new trees have been planted in Chinhae, and the festival continues to be observed, but now with a different focus. In modern Chinhae, the famed Admiral Yi Sunsin, who in the 16th century defeated Japanese soldiers in the Imjin War, is honored during the Cherry Blossom Festival with a parade, concerts, and folk games.

BUDDHA'S BIRTHDAY

In honor of Buddha's birthday, which falls on the eighth day of the fourth lunar month (sometime between late April and late May), Buddhists attend some of the numerous religious ceremonies and events held at temples throughout the country.

Once the state religion of the Korean peninsula, Buddhism fell from favor during the Choson dynasty. It was then that Confucianism replaced it as a social force. In spite of that, there are more Buddhists in Korea than followers of any other single religion.

On Buddha's birthday, colorful paper lanterns and flowers adorn the courtyards of temples. People congregate at temples to offer their prayers and hope for Buddha's blessing.

Many of these celebrants make their own lanterns and bring them to the temple. Others place flowers at the altar of the Buddha, or burn incense before the altar. In the evening, a lantern parade is held. The candlelight within the lanterns symbolizes hope.

Devout Buddhists offer prayers on Buddha's birthday. A sea of ancestors' name tags dangle from lanterns hung overhead.

어린이 만세

Children's Day celebration at a stadium. Usually held on a grand scale, the festivities traditionally include a band performance, dances, and martial arts demonstrations.

CHILDREN'S DAY

This holiday, which takes place on May 5 in South Korea and on June 6 in North Korea, originated during the Japanese occupation. It replaced what was previously known as Boys' Day. The new designation of Children's Day reflects a social consciousness that all children, not just boys, are to be treasured.

On this day children receive gifts from their parents, and they can usually choose the activities of the day. Youngsters often wear traditional dress when they visit the many public pageants and martial arts demonstrations held in their honor.

TAN-O DAY

Tan-O ("TAHN-oh") Day is also known as Swing Day and has been celebrated for centuries in Korea. It falls on the fifth day of the fifth lunar month, which is generally sometime between late May and late June.

This holiday originated as a day to pray for good harvests and is extremely important among rural people. According to ancient records, on this day people stopped their farming activities and threw a celebration similar to the New Year festivities.

Tan-O activities usually take place outdoors. In villages, people gather for outdoor events, whereas city dwellers usually get together in public parks and other outdoor meeting places where activities are held.

Dancing and puppet shows are popular pastimes on *Tan-O* Day. In addition, wrestling events are often scheduled for the men. The winner gets a bull as a prize.

Women and girls participate in swinging contests. The villages usually set up a long swing on the branch of an old tree, and the females of the town compete to see who can swing, standing up, to the highest height. The champion of this event sometimes gets a gold ring.

Silent mask dramas are also acted out in some regions. They are believed to drive away evil spirits.

Tan-O Day is especially important to rural folk as the grandeur of its celebration in the countryside proves.

111

A procession to grave sites on *Chusok*. It is a day when the moon is brightest and creativity flows.

CHUSOK

Chusok ("CHOO-suk"), the Harvest Moon Festival, is South Korea's Thanksgiving. It takes place on the 15th day of the eighth lunar month (early September to early October), when the moon is brightest. At *Chusok*, all Koreans try to return to their ancestral homes to attend memorial ceremonies in honor of their dead ancestors. Afterward, families set up an altar on a large table that also holds a banquet-like meal and burning incense.

A favorite traditional food on this day is a rice cake filled with bean paste or honey-sweetened sesame seeds. After the feast, Koreans dress in traditional clothing and visit graves to make food offerings and bow deeply to honor their ancestors. The festivities usually end with the viewing of the full moon along with poetry reading and writing. Koreans have long believed that the moon inspires their artistic nature.

CHRISTMAS

Korean Christians celebrate Christmas in much the same manner that Westerners do. Trees adorn homes, stores have extensive Christmas displays, and gifts are exchanged. There are church services on Christmas Eve, along with carolling, pageantry, and festive meals. Despite the growing numbers of Christians, Christmas is not a major holiday in Korea.

In South Korea

January 1–3	New Year's Day
February	Lunar New Year (Korean Traditional Folk Day)
	Tae-bo-rum (Great Moon Festival)
March 1	Independence Movement Day
March/April	Cherry Blossom Festival
April/May	Buddha's birthday
April 5	Arbor Day, a reforestation day when trees are planted
May 5	Children's Day
May/June	*Tan-O* Day
June 6	Memorial Day, a day of tribute to the war dead
July 17	Constitution Day
August 15	Liberation Day, anniversary of liberation from Japan in 1945
September /October	*Chusok* Day
October 3	National Foundation Day or Tangun Day, traditional founding of Korea by Tangun in 2333 B.C.
December 25	Christmas Day

In North Korea

January 1–2	New Year's Day
February 16	Birthday of the Dear Leader (Kim Jong Il); a day of celebration with cultural activities, sports events, and banquets
March 8	International Ladies' Day in socialist countries to commemorate the equality of women with men; on this day women are treated with special respect, particularly by their husbands, and receive presents
April 15	Birthday of the Great Leader (the late President Kim Il Sung), celebrated with nationwide cultural activities, sports events, and banquets
April 25	Army Day, to commemorate the founding of the People's Army
May 1	Labor Day
June 6	Children's Day
September 9	National Day, the anniversary of the founding of North Korea in 1948; state functions, political rallies, cultural activities, and sports activities mark this day
October 10	Party Foundation Day, the anniversary of the founding of the Korean Workers Party in 1945; a day for gatherings, speeches, and feasting

FOOD

"*PAM-MO-GO-SSO-YO* ("PAHM-moh-goh-soh-yoh")?" This is a Korean greeting, particularly popular in the countryside, that translates as, "Have you had rice today?" Rice is a staple of the Korean diet, and the question implies that if you have had rice you are okay, if not, food should be offered to you right away.

Apart from rice, Korean food can be easily distinguished from other Asian cuisines. The use of garlic, red pepper, green onion, sesame oil, and soy sauce, combined with the unique presentation, makes Korean food highly aromatic and easily identifiable.

Above: **Hot food being sold by a street vendor.**

Opposite: **People eating at Kukche Market, Pusan City. Note the low tables used even at street stalls.**

Koreans eat three meals a day, although the only distinction between breakfast, lunch, and dinner is the number of side dishes, or *panchan* ("bun-CHAHN"), served with each. As many as six dishes are prepared for breakfast, a dozen for the midday meal, and nearly 20 for the evening meal. Each meal generally includes rice; a traditional Korean pickle, or *kimchi* ("KIM-chee"), and soup, which is usually the only liquid taken with any meal. The soup may contain a number of ingredients, like beef, tofu, mung beansprouts, and other vegetables.

KIMCHI

Kimchi, a pickled, spicy vegetable dish, is Korea's best-known food. So closely is it associated with the national identity that it was declared a national treasure by the South Korean government. This fermented delicacy, which is said to be high in vitamins and nutrients, is served at every meal along with rice.

Culinary experts deem *kimchi* the king of pickles, for it ferments without vinegar. Although there are probably more than 200 varieties of this Korean delicacy, two kinds of *kimchi* are eaten in all homes: whole cabbage *kimchi* and hard radish *kimchi*. The whole cabbage variety consists of salted cabbage, sliced vegetables, herbs and spices, fermented fish sauce, fresh oysters, garlic, and chilies. The hard radish variety consists of cubed radish mixed with sliced cabbage and a few other vegetables. The predominant flavor of this spicy dish is red pepper.

In the summer, *kimchi* is made weekly because the vegetables are in season. But as winter approaches, *kimjang* ("KIM-jahng") begins. *Kimjang* is *kimchi*-making time. By the last weeks of November, when the weather has cooled and all the crops are in from the fields, the outdoor markets are burgeoning. Women across Korea start slicing, dicing, and spicing, preparing *kimchi* to last through the winter. This tradition began long ago, for once the bitter Korean winter sets in no crops can be produced until late spring.

Women gather in groups to cut, wash, and salt the hundreds of pounds of cabbage and white radish that are purchased for the winter supply. After it is prepared, *kimchi* is put into large earthenware crocks that are stored in the yard. In the countryside, when the temperature drops, the crocks are buried up to their necks to keep this favorite food from freezing.

Although refrigerators are now widely available in Korea, people still prefer to follow the *kimjang* tradition. A drive through any big city shows that even apartment dwellers place *kimchi* crocks out on the balcony.

So beloved is the classic dish that the world's only *kimchi* museum has been opened in Seoul, focusing on *kimchi's* history, lore, and numerous recipes.

USING CHOPSTICKS

Chopsticks are a challenge to anyone who is accustomed to knife and fork. But once the technique is understood and mastered, handling chopsticks is a breeze.

The trick to eating with chopsticks is to hold the stick closest to the palm very still, while moving the outside stick back and forth. The pair can then be used like pincers to grasp pieces of food.

The first chopstick should be tucked under the base of the thumb, with the lower part lightly resting on the inside of the ring finger. The second stick is then held like a pencil between thumb and forefinger. While holding the inner chopstick perfectly still, the outer chopstick can be moved forward and back. When the tips of the two sticks come together with some food in between, the hand should steadily bring the food thus pinched to the mouth. With a little practice, it's easy.

TABLE MANNERS

In a traditional Korean home, the men of the house are always served first, and the women must wait until they are no longer needed to replenish the dishes. After the men finish, the children and women eat. Sometimes the women and children eat in the kitchen while the men eat in the living room. In modern households, the whole family eats together.

Chopsticks and a soup spoon are set at each place. Once the meal has begun, the chopsticks are never to touch the table; it is customary to rest them on the rice bowl instead—not stuck in the rice, but placed across the bowl.

No one at the table is permitted to begin eating until the eldest person in the room has taken the first bite of food. Although there is little or no talking during meals, the room is hardly quiet. To show pleasure with the meal, slurping soup or noodles is customary. Also, older Koreans burp at the end of the meal to show satisfaction.

PULGOGI

Pulgogi is probably Korea's best-known dish next to *kimchi*. The thin strips of spicy grilled beef are loved by Koreans.

4 tablespoons soy sauce
2 tablespoons sesame oil
2 tablespoons sugar
$1/2$ teaspoon black pepper
1 clove garlic, finely chopped
4 tablespoons toasted sesame seeds
$1^1/2$ lbs ($^3/_4$ kg) sirloin tip, thinly sliced
12 leaves romaine lettuce
1 cup cooked rice
$^1/_8$ teaspoon cayenne pepper

In a large bowl, combine soy sauce, sesame oil, sugar, black pepper, garlic, and sesame seeds. Add meat and stir the mixture. Cover and refrigerate for 2 hours.

Light the barbecue or preheat oven to broil. Grill or broil meat for 2 to 3 minutes on each side.

Place a serving of meat on each lettuce leaf with 2 teaspoons of hot rice. Add a dash of cayenne pepper, then roll up the leaf.

TYPICAL MEALS

Other than the difference in the number of side dishes or *panchan*, the three daily meals in Korea all include rice, *kimchi*, soup, vegetables, and broiled or grilled fish or meat. Dessert is seldom served, but fruit in season is eaten after the meal.

Contrasts are important in Korean meals; bland rice goes well with a spicy dish, while cold salads are enjoyed with hot soups. The meals are also aesthetically pleasing, and often include the colors red, green, white, black, and yellow.

Traditionally, meals are served on a small, low table, with the food presented in neatly arranged little bowls. The table is set with a rice bowl in the middle, for rice is considered the main course. To the right of that is the soup bowl, and near the rice bowl various dishes of *panchan* are arranged, with several servings of each appearing on the table if many people are eating. The table is set in the kitchen before being carried out.

A typical Korean meal with the various side dishes laid out near the rice bowl.

Women sit beside the men at the table to make sure they have all they need as they eat.

ENTERTAINING GUESTS

Guests are lavishly entertained in Korean homes. Special foods are prepared and expense is no object, for it is a matter of great pride for Koreans to please guests. The hostess usually enjoys seeing her guests appreciate her food and the comfort of her home.

The meal is usually preceded by drinks served in the living room. The guests are then invited to eat—in the master bedroom. Those who are invited to a meal served in the bedroom know that they are indeed honored guests.

Low tables are placed end to end, with all the different dishes that are going to be served set out at the start. Before the meal begins, the host or hostess usually announces that the meal is humble, but the guests should eat a lot. This simply reflects the Korean belief that even the most sumptuous of feasts is not good enough for their honored guests. Despite the urging to eat a lot, guests must be certain to leave something in their bowls, otherwise the hostess may think that not enough food was served! And Koreans love guests to ask for more, since it is a sign that the food is sincerely appreciated.

Koreans do not talk much during meals; instead they concentrate on the delicious food. After the meal the dishes are cleared, then coffee and seasonal fruits are served. When alcohol is served, the men become quite uninhibited, so singing usually begins. The guest of honor is usually asked to sing the first song, and the merriment goes on for hours.

DRINKING CUSTOMS

The Koreans are avid drinkers and to drink alone is considered unacceptable in some areas. Traditionally, only men were permitted to drink in public, but now women are beginning to do so as well.

Strict rules prevail in Korean drinking. First of all, each person pours a drink for his fellow drinker but never for himself. Persons of lower status offer a glass to the most honored person, and if the status or age difference is significant, the glass is offered either with two hands or with the right hand supported by the left. The receiver also accepts the glass in the same way. Once the glass is in the receiver's hand, the giver pours the alcohol into it.

As each person finishes his own glass, it is the custom to pass the glass on until he has exchanged glasses with everyone else. Drinkers must be certain not to pour alcohol into a glass that is partially filled. If a person chooses not to drink at all, there is no problem, but refusing a drink after having started is considered antisocial behavior.

It is considered impolite in Korea to pour your own drink.

KOREA

RUSSIA

C H I N A

Legend:
- ● Capital city
- ● Major town
- ▲ Mountain Peak

Feet		Meters
16,500		5,000
9,900		3,000
6,600		2,000
3,300		1,000
1,650		500
660		200
0		0

Tumen

Mount Paektu
(9,003 ft/2,743 m)

Chongjin

Yalu

Kangnam Mountains

Changji

Myohyang Mts.

Kaema Plateau

Hamgyong Mountains

NORTH KOREA

Hamhung

Taedong

Nangnim Mountains

Sunan

Wonsan

Korea Bay

PYONGYANG

S e a   o f   J a p a n

Imjin

Mount Kumga ▲

Taebaek-San Maek

Mount Sorak ▲

Kaesong

Panmunjom

Kanghwa

SEOUL

Inchon

Han

SOUTH KOREA

N

Y e l l o w   S e a

Taejon

Sobaek Mountains

Naktong

Taegu

Kyongju

Kwangju

Chinhae

Pusan

Chin

Korea Strait

J A P A N

Cheju

Mount Halla
(6,398 ft / 1,949 m)

Cheju Island

Scale 1:5,850,000

0	25	50	75	100 Miles
0	50	100	150 Kilomete

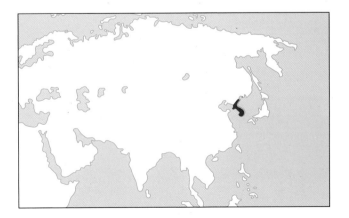

QUICK NOTES

NORTH KOREA

LAND AREA
47,399 square miles (122,763 square km)

POPULATION
23,067,000 (1994)

CAPITAL
Pyongyang

FLAG
The central red panel symbolizes the blood shed in liberating the country and the fighting spirit of the Korean people in support of their leader. The white circle and the two white lines indicate the homogeneity of the Koreans, while the red star depicts their bright future under the leadership of their revolutionary leader. The two horizontal blue lines reveal the desire to unite the revolutionary peoples of the world in their struggle for independence, friendship, and peace.

MAJOR RELIGIONS
Religious expression is not encouraged.

CURRENCY
Monetary unit—won
$1 = 2.15 won (Oct. 1994)

MAIN EXPORTS
Iron ore, steel, lead, zinc, and cement

HIGHEST POINT
Mount Paektu (9,003 feet / 2,743 meters)

SOUTH KOREA

LAND AREA
38,330 square miles (99,275 square km)

POPULATION
44,900,000 (1995)

CAPITAL
Seoul

FLAG
The white background of the *taeguk* (the South Korean flag, specifically the red and blue yin/yang) represents the land and the circle represents the people: upper red swirl, the males and the lower blue swirl, the females. The colors red and blue show the complementary nature of opposites like fire and water, light and dark. The three bars at each corner illustrate the balance of opposites. Starting with the upper left and moving clockwise, the three lines stand for heaven, earth, fire, and water.

MAJOR RELIGIONS
Buddhism, Taoism, and Christianity

CURRENCY
Monetary unit—won
$1 = 779 won (Oct. 1994)

MAIN EXPORTS
Textiles, electronic and electrical equipment, footwear, and automobiles

HIGHEST POINT
Mount Halla (6,398 feet / 1,949 meters)

GLOSSARY

chaebol ("JAE-bull")
A business conglomerate.

chungmae ("choong-MAY")
Arranged marriage.

haenyo ("hay-NIO")
Women divers on Cheju Island.

ham ("HAHM")
A box of gifts for the bride, sent by the groom as part of the wedding ritual.

hanbok ("HUN-bok")
Traditional Korean dress.

hangul ("HAHN-gool")
The Korean phonetic writing system.

ho-juk ("HOH-juck")
Family registers used to help trace ancestry.

hwangap ("HWUN-gup")
Sixtieth birthday celebration.

juche (CHOO-cheh")
Self-reliance.

kibun ("KEY-boon")
Social harmony.

kimchi ("KIM-chee")
A traditional Korean pickle.

kisaeng ("KEY-sang")
A female entertainer, usually a talented poet, singer, or musician.

kumjul ("KEHM-jool")
A straw rope of chili peppers hung across the doorway of a house to frighten off evil spirits and warn people not to enter because a baby has just been born.

kut ("KOOD")
A ceremony to exorcise evil spirits.

mudang ("MOO-dung")
Shaman, or spirit medium.

nunchi ("NOON-chi")
An intuition or hunch that lets a person "read" another person's state of mind.

panchan ("bun-CHAHN")
The side dishes that accompany every Korean meal.

ondol ("ON-doll")
Heating system: floors heated by hot air running through pipes beneath the floor.

Samshin Halmoni ("SUM-shin Hul-MO-neh")
The grandmother spirit associated with childbirth.

sijo ("SAE-jo")
A form of traditional Korean poetry.

Sol-nal ("SUHL-nahl")
Lunar New Year.

tol ("DOUL")
A child's first birthday.

BIBLIOGRAPHY

Farley, Carol. *Land of the Morning Calm*. New York: Macmillan Children's Book Group, 1991.

Macdonald, Donald S. *The Koreans: Contemporary Politics and Society*. Revised edition. Boulder, Colorado: Westview Press, 1990.

Nash, Amy. *North Korea*. New York: Chelsea House, 1991.

Rucci, Richard, B., ed. American Chamber of Commerce in Korea: *Living In Korea*. 2d. rev. ed., Seoul: Seoul International Tourist Publishing, 1981.

Savada, Andrea Matles. *South Korea: A Country Study*. Washington, D.C.: U.S. Government Printing Office, 1992.

Savada, Andrea Matles. *North Korea: A Country Study*. Washington, D.C.: U.S. Government Printing Office, 1994.

Solberg, Sammy E. *The Land and People of Korea*. New York: Harper Collins, 1991.

South Korea in Pictures. Minneapolis, MN: Department of Geography, Lerner Publications, 1989.

INDEX

INDEX

INDEX

PICTURE CREDITS
R. L'Anson: 13, 38, 39, 79
APA: 5, 12, 27, 28, 36, 40 (bottom), 44,
   49 (bottom), 51, 57, 60, 95, 114, 121
Camera Press: 35
Embassy of the Democratic People's
   Republic of Korea: 40 (top)
Embassy of the Republic of Korea: 34
Hutchison Library: 23, 24, 25, 26, 32,
   52, 56 (top), 58, 59, 68, 75, 84, 87,
   90, 109, 110, 118
Image Bank: 3, 15, 19, 30, 33, 46 (top),
   48, 54, 78, 81
B. Klingwall: 6, 9, 16, 17, 20, 22 (top),
   29, 31, 37, 49 (top), 50, 56 (bottom),
   61, 83, 97, 119
Korean National Tourism Corporation:
   4, 7, 10, 11, 14 (top and bottom),
   18, 22 (bottom), 45, 46 (bottom) 53,
   62, 64, 66, 67, 69, 70, 71, 72, 73, 74,
   76, 85, 86, 88, 89, 91, 93, 94, 96, 99,
   100, 101, 102, 103, 104, 105, 106, 107,
   108, 111, 112, 117 (top and bottom),
   120, 123
Life File: 43, 115
B. Sonneville: 1, 47, 82